AMERICA'S NONPROFIT SECTOR

A PRIMER

AMERICA'S NONPROFIT SECTOR

A PRIMER

Lester M. Salamon
The Johns Hopkins University

The Foundation Center

Library of Congress Cataloging-in-Publication Data

Salamon, Lester M.
    America's nonprofit sector : a primer / Lester M. Salamon.
        p.   cm.
    Includes bibliographical references (p.   ).
    ISBN 0-87954-451-1 : $14.95
    1. Charities—United States. 2. Corporations, Nonprofit—United
States. 3. Human Services—United States. 4. Public welfare-
-United States.   I. Title.
    HV91.S23 1992
    361.7'0973—dc20   92-11083
                                                              CIP

For
Noah and Matt

Table of Contents

List of
Tables and Figures

ACKNOWLEDGMENTS

The inspiration for this monograph was a request from David Tobin and Robert Smucker of Independent Sector, the Washington-based umbrella group representing the nation's nonprofit organizations, for a basic, easy-to-understand handbook that could help members of Congress, governors, mayors, and other public officials and interpreters of public affairs understand the scope and scale of America's private nonprofit sector and the role that it plays in our national life.

With the recent democratic breakthroughs in Eastern Europe, and the surge of interest in the nonprofit sector in other parts of the world as well, a new objective was added to the project: to provide a basic introduction to the American nonprofit sector that could help those interested in such organizations overseas understand what this sector is all about and how it fits into American society.

Whatever merits the resulting work possesses owes much to the diligent and effective research assistance of Ms. Gretchen van Fossan, to the helpful advice and encouragement of David Tobin and Robert Smucker, to the useful comments of Virginia Hodgkinson and Murray Weitzman of Independent Sector, and to the assistance of the many government officials who provided data and reports and responded to numerous queries about inconsistencies in different data systems. I also want to express my gratitude to Independent Sector and to the Rockefeller Brothers Fund for financial support that helped make this project possible.

Any shortcomings the work contains, and any opinions and views expressed, however, are my responsibility alone, and are not necessarily shared by any individual or organization with which I am affiliated or that has supported this work.

It is my hope that this primer will provide a solid, factual picture of the significant role that nonprofit organizations play in American society, the way these organizations are financed, and the trends that have recently affected them so that people in this country and abroad can approach these organizations free of the myths and ideology that have too often characterized public discussions about them. Only in this way will the true importance of these organizations become apparent.

Lester M. Salamon
Baltimore, Maryland
June 1992

Preface

Those of us interested in the future of the private nonprofit sector have been concerned about the lack of understanding of this set of organizations among both national leaders and the general public. One of the most serious obstacles has been the lack of solid information that can help make this sector's role and impact clearer to those whose support is so essential to its capacity to be of continuing and growing service to society. With the publication of Lester Salamon's *America's Nonprofit Sector: A Primer,* an essential resource is finally at hand.

A pioneering researcher on the nonprofit sector and on public policy, Salamon has produced an extraordinarily lucid account of America's nonprofit sector—its purposes, character, usefulness, and limitations. Beyond that, he has assembled extensive and fascinating information to provide a unique picture of the relative roles of nonprofit organizations, for-profit businesses, and government in serving human needs and promoting cultural and civic life in our country. And he presents it in ways that are precise, readable, and engaging.

For those who need to know more about this field, Salamon's *Primer* is extemely useful. It explains what the nonprofit sector is and why we have it, how big this sector is, how it is financed, the relationship between the nonprofit sector and government, and the development of government policy in key social welfare fields. It also takes the reader through each of the many fields where nonprofit organizations are active—health, education, social services, arts and culture, international aid, advocacy, legal aid—and shows how the nonprofit sector compares to government and for-profit institutions in number, revenues, and employment, and how these relationships have evolved. Policymakers in local and national government, board members of nonprofit organizations, nonprofit executives, foundation officials, and students of American social policy and public administration will find this a valuable introduction to a world that has remained far too obscure for far too long.

Even long-time students of the field will find much to learn in this account. For example, Salamon shows that the scale of nonprofit activity is very close to that of government action in the fields where both are involved, and that in fact the levels of nonprofit expenditures in some fields outdistance those of either the Federal government or state and local governments, if taken separately. Quite apart from their social and civic values, nonprofit organizations represent an immense economic force in our society that alone justifies taking them more seriously than we have.

Also revealing is Salamon's documentation of such recent trends as:

- The growing importance of fee income in the financing of nonprofit activity;
- the disproportionate growth of for-profit firms in a number of traditional fields of nonprofit activity—such as, hospitals, outpatient clinics, and social services;
- the significant growth of private giving during the 1980s.

Salamon's account is not intended to celebrate the independent sector or to criticize it. His intention is to describe and explain it and thereby provide a basis for objective analysis. In this, he succeeds superbly. He has given us a landmark account of a critical area of our national life that has remained in the shadows for too long.

Brian O'Connell
President, Independent Sector
Washington, DC
March 30, 1992

Introduction

Modern societies, whatever their politics, have found it necessary to make special provisions to protect individuals against the vagaries of economic misfortune, old age, and disability; and to secure basic human rights.

Because of the complexities of modern urban life, what could be handled at an earlier time, however imperfectly, by a combination of self-reliance, spontaneous neighborliness, and family ties has required more institutionalized forms of help in modern times.

How this need is met, however, varies widely from place to place. In some countries, governments have guaranteed their citizens a minimum income, and a minimum level of health care, housing, and other necessities of life. In others, private corporations or private charitable institutions shoulder a far larger share of the responsibility for coping with human needs. And in still others, complex, mixed systems of aid are in force, combining elements of public and private provision, collective and individual responsibility.

In few countries is the system of aid more complicated and confusing, however, than in the United States. Reflecting a deep-seated tradition of individualism and an ingrained hostility to centralized institutions, Americans have resisted the worldwide movement toward exclusively governmental approaches to social welfare provision, adding new governmental provisions only with great reluctance, and then structuring them in ways that preserve a substantial private role.

The result is an intricate "mixed economy" of welfare that blends public and private action in ways that few people truly understand. In truth, the resulting system is not a system at all, but an ad hoc collec-

"The purpose of this primer is to overcome [the] widespread lack of knowledge about America's nonprofit sector and the role it plays in our social welfare system."

"The American social welfare system is, in truth, not a system at all, but an ad hoc collection of compromises between the realities of economic necessity and the pressures of political tradition and ideology."

tion of compromises between the realities of economic necessity and the pressures of political tradition and ideology.

One of the more important and distinctive features of the American approach to social welfare provision is the important role it leaves to private, nonprofit organizations, to nongovernmental institutions that nevertheless serve essentially public, as opposed to private economic, goals. Of all the components of our social welfare system, this is the one that is most commonly misunderstood and about which the least is known.

The purpose of this "primer" is to overcome this widespread lack of knowledge about America's nonprofit sector and the role it plays in our mixed economy. To do so, however, it is necessary not only to examine the scope, scale, and structure of the nonprofit sector, but also to assess the scale and range of government and private business involvement in the same fields since these three sectors are all integral parts of the "mixed economy" that exists. In other words, this primer seeks to answer questions such as the following:

- What are nonprofit organizations, what features do they have in common, and why do they exist?
- What different types of nonprofit organizations are there and what is the scale of each major type?
- Where do nonprofit organizations get their funds?
- How extensive is government social welfare spending in the fields in which nonprofit organizations are active? Is it true, as many people believe, that government spending vastly outdistances nonprofit spending in these fields?
- What role do nonprofit organizations play in the various fields in which they are involved? For example:
  - What share of all hospital beds are in nonprofit hospitals as compared to government hospitals or private, not-for-profit hospitals?
  - What proportion of all home health facilities are nonprofits as opposed to for-profits?
  - What share of all colleges and universities are nonprofits and what proportion of all students enrolled in colleges or universities are enrolled in nonprofit institutions as opposed to public (governmental) ones?
  - What have been the recent trends in the relative importance of nonprofit, for-profit, and government providers in these various fields? Are nonprofits generally gaining ground or losing it?

To answer these and related questions, the discussion that follows falls into three major sections containing ten chapters in all. The four chapters that comprise Section I provide a broad overview of the nonprofit sector and its role in the American social

"One of the more important and distinctive features of the American approach to social welfare provision is the important role it leaves to private, nonprofit organizations...."

welfare system. The first chapter in this section defines more precisely what a nonprofit organization is and explores the basic rationale for this type of organization. Chapter 2 examines the anatomy of the American nonprofit sector, identifying the major components and the overall scale and scope of each one. In Chapter 3 attention turns to the *governmental role* in the American social welfare system and the relationship between governmental activity and the activity of the nonprofit sector. Chapter 4 puts current realities into historical context, reviewing the way this system evolved and the recent trends to which it has been exposed.

Against this backdrop, Section II then looks more closely at the role of the nonprofit sector in each of the major subfields in which it operates—health, education, social services, arts and culture, advocacy and international aid. For each, an attempt is made to identify the role of the nonprofit sector, to compare it to the roles played by government and private, for-profit firms, and to identify recent trends. A final section then provides some summary observations.

Clearly no work of this scale can offer a full-scale evaluation of how well our social welfare system is working or what the advantages and disadvantages of nonprofit organizations are. The conscious attempt here, therefore, is to be largely descriptive, to portray the major components of this complex system and show how they fit together, and to do so in as accessible and nontechnical a fashion as possible.

Even this modest objective poses serious challenges, however, which perhaps explains why it has never been attempted before. No single data source compiles systematic information on all the various facets of our social welfare system broken down by sector. What is more, various data sources covering similar aspects of the field often provide widely varying estimates because of subtle differences in definitions and coverage. Thus, for example, an annual estimate of government spending on health compiled by the Social Security Administration yields an estimate that differs considerably from the estimate that the Health Care Financing Administration provides in its annual summary of "national health expenditures." Total spending by hospitals as reported in the "national health expenditures" series is in turn hard to reconcile with the independent estimates provided at five-year intervals in the U.S. Census Bureau's *Census of Service Industries* or the annual surveys conducted by the American Hospital Association. Assembling a full picture of the scope of nonprofit activity and how it compares to the scope of government and business activity in each of the major subfields of our social welfare system is therefore a Herculean task, requiring careful sifting of dozens of different data sources and reconciliation of hundreds of definitional

"Assembling a full picture of the scope of nonprofit activity and how it compares to the scope of government and business activity in each of the major subfields of our social welfare system is...a Herculean task, requiring careful sifting of dozens of different data sources and reconciliation of hundreds of definitional and empirical anomalies."

and empirical anomalies.

Though complicated, however, such an effort is well worth undertaking, and not just for descriptive reasons. In addition:

- It can better equip both policymakers and the citizenry at large to understand a system that has long seemed to defy comprehension.
- It can clarify the role of the long-overlooked nonprofit sector and bring this sector into focus for the first time.
- It can introduce non-Americans to the important role that nonprofit organizations play in our social and political life.
- It can thus enable all concerned to make more sensible policy choices.

If this work satisfies even some of these objectives, it will have served its purpose well.

ENDNOTES

1. Other accounts provide useful information on the American nonprofit sector, but none of these systematically compares the nonprofit sector to other components of our mixed economy both in general and in particular subfields. See, for example: Waldemar A. Nielsen, *The Endangered Sector* (New York: Columbia University Press, 1979); Michael O'Neill, *The Third America: The Emergence of the Nonprofit Sector in the United States* (San Francisco: Jossey-Bass Publishers, 1989); and Virginia A. Hodgkinson, Murray S. Weitzman, and Stephen M. Noga, *The Nonprofit Almanac, 1992-1993: Dimensions of the Independent Sector,* (San Francisco, CA: Jossey-Bass Publishers,Inc., 1992).

PART ONE

Overview

CHAPTER ONE

What is the Nonprofit Sector and Why Do We Have It?

Nothing, in my opinion, is more deserving of our attention than the intellectual and moral associations of America.
    ALEXIS DE TOQUEVILLE, 1835

Few aspects of American society are as poorly understood or as obscured by mythology as the thousands of day-care centers, clinics, hospitals, higher-education institutions, civic action groups, museums, symphonies, and related organizations that comprise America's private, nonprofit sector.

More than a century and a half ago, the Frenchman Alexis de Toqueville identified this sector as one of the most distinctive and critical features of American life. Yet, despite a steady diet of charitable appeals, most Americans know precious little about the sector or what it does. Indeed, to judge from press accounts and national policy debates, it would seem as if the nonprofit sector largely disappeared from the American scene some 60 years ago, as both public and scholarly attention focused instead on government policy and the expansion of the State.

In fact, however, as the third century of the American democratic experiment begins, the private, nonprofit sector remains at least as potent a component of American life as it was when de Toqueville observed it more than a century and a half ago. This sector contains some of the most prestigious and important institutions in American society—Harvard University, the Metropolitan Museum of Art, the NAACP, to name just a few (see Table 1.1). More than that, it engages the activities and enlists the support of literally millions of citizens, providing a mechanism for self-help, for voluntary assistance to those in need, and for the pursuit of a wide array of interests and beliefs. Finally, this sector has helped give rise to a distinctively American version of the modern welfare state, which features extensive interaction between government and nonprofit groups to help respond to public needs.[1] In fact, without a clear understanding of the nonprofit sector, it is as impossi-

"...as the third century of the American democratic experiment begins, the private, nonprofit sector remains at least as potent a component of American life as it was when de Toqueville observed it more than a century and a half ago."

TABLE 1.1

Sample Nonprofit Organizations

Harvard University
Princeton University
Montefiore Hospital
American Red Cross
American Cancer Society
Boy Scouts of America
Girl Scouts of America
Rockefeller Foundation
N.Y. Philharmonic Orchestra
Folger Theater
Metropolitan Museum of Art
Planned Parenthood
Catholic Relief Services
C.A.R.E.
Audubon Society
Environmental Defense Fund
National Association for the Advancement
    of Colored People (NAACP)
The Brookings Institution
American Enterprise Institute

TABLE 1.2

Types of Tax-Exempt Organizations under U.S. Law

Tax Code Number	Type of Tax-exempt Organization
501(c)(1)	Corporations organized under an act of Congress
501(c)(2)	Title-holding companies
501(c)(3)	Religious, charitable, educational, etc.
501(c)(4)	Social welfare
501(c)(5)	Labor, agriculture organization
501(c)(6)	Business leagues
501(c)(7)	Social and recreational clubs
501(c)(8)	Fraternal beneficiary societies
501(c)(9)	Voluntary employees' beneficiary societies
501(c)(10)	Domestic fraternal beneficiary societies
501(c)(11)	Teachers' retirement fund
501(c)(12)	Benevolent life insurance associations
501(c)(13)	Cemetery companies
501(c)(14)	Credit unions
501(c)(15)	Mutual insurance companies
501(c)(16)	Corporations to finance crop operation
501(c)(17)	Supplemental unemployment benefit trusts
501(c)(18)	Employee-funded pension trusts
501(c)(19)	War veterans' organizations
501(c)(20)	Legal services organizations
501(c)(21)	Black lung trusts
501(d)	Religious and apostolic organizations
501(e)	Cooperative hospital service organizations
501(f)	Cooperative service organizations of operating educational organizations
521	Farmers' cooperatives

Source: Internal Revenue Service, Annual Report

ble to comprehend American society and American public policy today as it was in the time of de Toqueville.

What is the Nonprofit Sector?

But what is this "nonprofit sector"? What is it that the organizations that are part of this sector have in common? Why do we have such organizations? What purpose do they serve?

A Diverse Sector

Unfortunately, the answers to these questions are somewhat complicated because of the great diversity of this sector. U.S. tax laws contain no fewer than 26 separate sections under which organizations can claim exemption from federal income taxes as nonprofit organizations. Mutual insurance companies, certain cooperatives, labor unions, business leagues, as well as charitable and educational institutions are all eligible (see Table 1.2). Of these, the "religious, charitable, and educational" organizations eligible for tax exemption under Section 501(c)(3) are probably the best known—yet included even within this narrow span are a wide assortment of institutions:

- small, one-room soup kitchens for the homeless;
- massive hospital complexes;
- museums, art galleries, and symphony orchestras;
- day-care centers;
- foster care and adoption agencies; and
- advocacy and civic action groups bringing pressure on government and the private sector to clean the environment, protect farmers, promote civil rights, or pursue a thousand other causes.

The Terminological Tangle

Nor does the terminology used to depict the sector provide much help. A great many such terms are used—*nonprofit sector, charitable sector, independent sector, voluntary sector,* and *tax-exempt sector.* Each of these terms emphasizes one aspect of the reality represented by these organizations at the expense of overlooking or downplaying other aspects. Each is therefore at least partly misleading. For example:

- *Charitable sector* emphasizes the support these organizations receive from private, charitable donations. But as we shall see, private charitable contributions do not constitute the only, or even the major, source of their revenue.
- *Independent sector* emphasizes the important role these organizations play as a "third force" outside of the realm of government and private business. But as we shall see, these organizations are far from

independent. In financial terms they depend heavily on both government and private business.

- *Voluntary sector* emphasizes the significant input that volunteers make to the management and operation of this sector. But as we shall see, most of the activity of the organizations in this sector is not carried out by volunteers at all, but by paid employees.

- *Tax-exempt sector* emphasizes the fact that under U.S. tax law, the organizations in this sector are exempt from the national income tax and from most state and local property taxes. But this term begs the question of what characteristics qualify organizations for this treatment in the first place. In addition, it is not very helpful in comparing U.S. experience with that elsewhere because it is so dependent on the peculiarities of U.S. tax law.

- Even *nonprofit sector*, the term we will generally use here, is not without its problems. This term emphasizes the fact that these organizations do not exist primarily to generate profits for their owners. But as we shall see, these organizations sometimes do earn profits, that is, they generate more revenues than they spend in a given year.

A Crucial Distinction: Philanthropy versus the Nonprofit Sector

The task of comprehending the nonprofit sector is further complicated by a widespread failure to recognize the important distinction between *philanthropy,* on the one hand, and t*he private, nonprofit sector,* on the other. In many accounts, these two terms are treated interchangeably when in fact one is really just a part of the other.

- The *private nonprofit sector,* as the term will be used here, is a set of organizations that is privately incorporated but serving some public purpose, such as the advancement of health, education, scientific progress, social welfare, or pluralism. The nonprofit sector thus includes thousands of day-care centers, private hospitals, universities, research institutes, community development organizations, foster care facilities, social service agencies, employment and training centers, museums, art galleries, symphonies, zoos, business and professional associations, advocacy organizations, and dozens of similar types of institutions.

- *Philanthropy* is the giving of gifts of time or valuables (money, securities, property) for public purposes. Philanthropy, or charitable giving, is thus one form of income of private nonprofit organizations. To be sure, some nonprofit organizations have the generation of charitable contributions as

"The task of comprehending the nonprofit sector is further complicated by a widespread failure to recognize the important distinction between philanthropy, *on the one hand, and* the private, nonprofit sector, *on the other. In many accounts, these two terms are treated interchangeably when in fact one is really just a part of the other."*

5

TABLE 1.3

Six Defining Characteristics of the Nonprofit Sector

The nonprofit sector is a collection of organizations that are
1. formally constituted;
2. private, as opposed to governmental;
3. not profit-distributing;
4. self-governing;
5. voluntary; and
6. of public benefit.

their principal objective. But as we will see, these are not the only types of nonprofit organizations, and private charitable contributions are not the only source of nonprofit income.

Six Defining Characteristics

What, then, do the organizations that comprise the "nonprofit sector" have in common? What are the defining characteristics of this sector?

Broadly speaking, six characteristics seem most crucial (see Table 1.3).[2] In particular, as we will use the term here, the nonprofit sector refers to a set of organizations that are:

- *Formal,* that is, institutionalized to some extent. Purely ad hoc, informal, and temporary gatherings of people are not considered part of the nonprofit sector, even though they may be quite important in people's lives. At the same time, the nonprofit sector may include many organizations that are not formally incorporated. Typically, however, nonprofit organizations have a legal identity as corporations chartered under state laws. This corporate status makes the organization a legal person able to enter contracts and largely frees the officers of personal financial responsibility for the organization's commitments.

- *Private,* that is, institutionally separate from government. Nonprofit organizations are neither part of the governmental apparatus nor governed by boards dominated by government officials. This does not mean that they may not receive significant government support. What is more, government participation on nonprofit boards is not unheard of, as was the case with Yale University until the 1870s.[3] But nonprofit organizations are fundamentally private institutions in basic structure.

- *Non-profit-distributing,* that is, not dedicated to generating profits for their owners. Nonprofit organizations may accumulate profits in a given year, but the profits must be plowed back into the basic mission of the agency, not distributed to the organizations' founders. This differentiates nonprofit organizations from the other component of the private sector—private businesses.

- *Self-governing,* that is, equipped to control their own activities. Nonprofit organizations have their own internal procedures for governance and are not controlled by outside entities.

- *Voluntary,* that is, involving some meaningful degree of voluntary participation, either in the actual conduct of the agency's activities or in the management of its affairs. Typically, this takes the form of a voluntary board of directors, but exten-

sive use of volunteer staff is also common.
- *Of public benefit*, that is, serving some public purpose and contributing to the public good.

The Rationale:
Why Do We Have a Nonprofit Sector?

Why does the nonprofit sector exist in the United States, or any other country? Why did such organizations come into existence, and why do we give these organizations special tax and other advantages?

Five major considerations seem to be involved.

Historical

In the first place, the nonprofit sector came into existence for reasons that are largely historical. In the United States, as well as in many other countries, society predated the state. In other words, communities formed before governmental structures, or governmental institutions, were in place to help deal with their common concerns. People therefore had to tackle problems on their own and often found it useful to join with others in voluntary organizations to do so. The result was the creation of voluntary fire departments, schools, adoption societies, and many more. Even after governments came into existence, moreover, Americans were often reluctant to use them, fearing the rebirth of monarchy, or bureaucracy. Therefore, citizens still had to take matters into their own hands until they could persuade their fellow citizens that government help was needed. Once created, these organizations then often continued in existence even after government entered the scene, frequently helping government meet a need.

Market Failure

Beyond this historical reason, the creation of nonprofit organizations has been motivated by certain inherent limitations of the market system, which dominates the American economy.[4] Economists refer to these as *market failures*. Essentially, the problem is this: The market is excellent for handling those things we consume individually, such as shoes, cars, clothing, food. For such items, consumer choices in the marketplace send signals to producers about the prices that will be paid and the quantities that can be sold at those prices. By contrast, the market does not handle very well those things that can only be consumed collectively, such as clean air, national defense, or safe neighborhoods. These so-called public goods involve a serious "free-rider" problem because, once they are produced, everyone can benefit from them even if they have not shared in the cost. Therefore, it is to each individual's advantage to let his or her neighbor bear the cost of these collective goods because each individual will be able to enjoy them whether he or she pays for them or not. Because everyone will think the same way, however, the inevitable result will be to produce far too little of these collective goods and thus leave everyone worse off.

To correct for this, some form of nonmarket mechanism is needed. One such mechanism is government. By imposing taxes on individuals, government can compel everyone to share in the cost of collective goods. But another mechanism for overcoming market failure is the nonprofit sector. Nonprofit organizations allow groups of individuals to pool their resources to produce collective goods they mutually desire but cannot convince a majority of their countrymen to support. This can happen, for example, when particular subgroups share certain cultural, social, or economic characteristics or interests not shared by all citizens of a country. Through nonprofit organizations such subgroups can provide the kinds and levels of collective goods they desire.

A slightly different kind of market failure occurs where the purchasers of services are not the same as the consumers, a situation economists refer to as *contract failure*.[5] This is the case, for example, with nursing homes, where the consumers are often elderly people with limited consumer choice or ability to discriminate among products and the purchasers are their children. In such situations, the purchasers, unable to assess the adequacy of services themselves, seek some substitute for the market mechanism, some provider they can trust. Because nonprofits do not exist principally to earn profits, they often are preferred providers in such situations.

Government Failure

A third reason for the existence of a vibrant nonprofit sector springs from certain inherent limitations of government as a provider of collective goods. In the first place, in a democracy it is often difficult to get government to act to correct "market failures" because government action requires majority support. By forming nonprofit organizations, smaller groupings of people can begin addressing needs that they have not yet convinced others to support.

Even when majority support exists, however, there is still often a preference for some nongovernmental mechanism to deliver services and respond to public needs because of the cumbersomeness, unresponsiveness, and bureaucratization that often accompanies government action. This is particularly true in the United States because of a strong cultural resistance to the expansion of government. Even when government financing is viewed as essential, therefore, it is

"In democratic countries the science of association is the mother of science; the progress of all the rest depends on the progress it has made."

often the case that private, nonprofit organizations are utilized to deliver the services that government finances. The result, as will be detailed later, is a complex pattern of cooperation between government and the nonprofit sector.

Pluralism/Freedom

A fourth reason for the existence of nonprofit organizations has less to do with the efficiency of these organizations or the service functions they perform than with the role they play in promoting a crucial social value—the value of freedom and pluralism. As John Stuart Mill pointed out in his classic treatise, *On Liberty*, "Government operations tend to be everywhere alike. With individuals and voluntary associations, on the contrary, there are varied experiments, and endless diversity of experience."[6] Nonprofit organizations encourage individual initiative for the public good just as the business corporation encourages individual action for the private good. Most of the major reforms in American society, in fact, have originated in this nonprofit sector—civil rights, environmental protection, workplace safety, child welfare, women's rights, and the New Right. Even if it were the case that government was far more efficient than the nonprofit sector in responding to citizen needs, Americans would still insist on a vibrant nonprofit sector as a guarantor of their liberties and a mechanism to ensure a degree of pluralism.

Solidarity

Finally, the nonprofit sector is a response to the need for some mechanism through which to give expression to sentiments of solidarity. This is particularly important in individualistic societies like the United States, as Alexis de Toqueville pointed out in his seminal essay 150 years ago. In fact, it was this facet of the nonprofit sector that Toqueville had principally in mind when he argued, "In democratic countries the science of association is the mother of science; the progress of all the rest depends upon the progress it has made."[7] The reason, Toqueville observed, is that "...among democratic nations...all the citizens are independent and feeble; they can do hardly anything by themselves, and none of them can oblige his fellow men to lend him their assistance. They all, therefore, become powerless if they do not learn voluntarily to help one another."

Voluntary associations are thus needed especially critically in democratic societies to create artificially what the equality of conditions makes it extremely difficult to create naturally, namely, a capacity for joint action. It is for this reason that Toqueville finds it so noteworthy that "wherever at the head of some

"If men living in democratic countries had no right and no inclination to associate for political purposes, their independence would be in great jeopardy, but they might long preserve their wealth and their cultivation; whereas if they never acquired the habit of forming associations in ordinary life, civilization itself would be endangered."
ALEXIS DE TOQUEVILLE

new undertaking you see government in France, or a man of rank in England, in the United States you will be sure to find an association." As he notes, "If men living in democratic countries had no right and no inclination to associate for political purposes, their independence would be in great jeopardy, but they might long preserve their wealth and their cultivation; whereas if they never acquired the habit of forming associations in ordinary life, civilization itself would be endangered."

Conclusion

In short, there is a vitally important set of institutions in American society that, despite many differences, all share certain common features. They are formally constituted, private, self-governing, non-profit-distributing, voluntary, and of public benefit. Together they comprise what we will call the nonprofit sector.

The existence of this set of organizations is partly an accident of history. But it has more concrete foundations as well—in the inherent limitations of the market in responding to public needs, in the inherent limitations of government as the sole alternative mechanism to respond to market failures, in the need that a democratic society has for some way to promote cooperation among equal individuals, and in the value Americans attach to pluralism and freedom.

The rationale for the existence of a nonprofit sector is not peculiar to American society, of course. The same arguments apply to other societies as well, particularly those with democratic governmental structures and market-oriented economic systems. But there is no denying that these organizations have come to play a particularly important role in the American setting. While there is reason to question whether American nonprofit organizations always live up to the expectations that these theories assign to them, it seems clear that the existence of such a set of institutions has come to be viewed as a critical component of community life, a compelling and fulfilling way to meet community needs, and a crucial prerequisite of a true "civil society."

"...the existence of a set of institutions that is private, nonprofit, and self-governing has come to be viewed in this country both as a convenient and fulfilling way to meet community needs and as a crucial prerequisite of a true 'civil society.'"

ENDNOTES

1. This pattern is, of course, not unique to America. For other examples of countries that have built extensive reliance on the nonprofit sector into their social welfare systems, see the chapters on Germany and the Netherlands in Benjamin Gidron, Ralph Kramer, and Lester M. Salamon, eds., *Government and the Third Sector: Emerging Relationships in Welfare States* (San Francisco: Jossey-Bass, 1992).

2. Maria Brenton, *The Voluntary Sector in British Social Services* (London: Longman, 1985), p. 9.

3. John S. Whitehead, *The Separation of College and State: Columbia, Dartmouth, Harvard and Yale,* 1776-1876 (New Haven, CT: Yale University Press, 1973).

4. This line of argument has been applied to the nonprofit sector most explicitly in Burton Weisbrod, *The Voluntary Nonprofit Sector* (Lexington, MA: Lexington Books, 1978).

5. This line of argument has been developed most explicitly in Henry Hansmann, "Why Are Nonprofit Organizations Exempted from Corporate Income Taxation," in Michelle J. White (ed.), *Nonprofit Firms in a Three-Sector Economy*, COUPE Papers (Washington, DC: The Urban Institute Press, 1981).

6. John Stuart Mill, *On Liberty*, quoted in Bruce R. Hopkins, *The Law of Tax-Exempt Organizations*, 5th Ed. (New York: John Wiley and Sons, 1987), p. 7.

7. Alexis deToqueville, *Democracy in America* [The Henry Reeve Text] (New York: Alfred A. Knopf, Inc., 1945), pp. 114-118.

Scope and Structure: The Anatomy of America's Nonprofit Sector

To say that nonprofit organizations share certain common characteristics and a common rationale is not, of course, to suggest that all nonprofit organizations are identical. To the contrary, the complexity and diversity of this sector is one of the major factors that has diverted attention from it over much of its history. Nonprofit organizations are so diverse and so specialized in the United States that some observers question whether it is appropriate to consider this group of institutions a sector at all.

The purpose of this chapter is to make some sense of the vast array of institutional types that comprise the American nonprofit sector, to examine the basic anatomy or architecture of this sector and the scope and scale of some of its constituent parts. In the process, it seeks to strip away some of the confusion and misperception that too often characterizes popular understanding of what the nonprofit sector really is and how it functions in American life.

To do so, we first identify some of the basic divisions within the nonprofit sector and then examine in more detail some of its major components, focusing particularly on what we refer to as "public-benefit service organizations," which is what most people have in mind when they refer to the "nonprofit sector."

A Basic Division: Public-Serving versus Member-Serving Organizations

Perhaps the most basic point to realize about the nonprofit sector is that the approximately 1.1 million organizations that constitute it in the United States at the present time include two very different categories of organizations.

FIGURE 2.1
Anatomy of the Nonprofit Sector

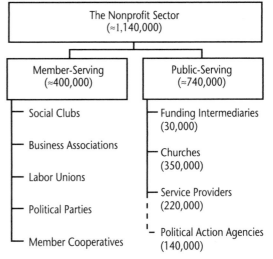

Source: Author's estimates based on data in *Report of the Commissioner of Internal Revenue* (Washington: U.S. Government Printing Office, 1989).

Member-Serving Organizations

The first are what we refer to as *primarily member-serving* organizations. These are organizations that, while having some public purpose, primarily exist to provide a benefit to the members of the organization rather than to the public at large. As reflected in Figure 2.1, the member-serving organizations include social clubs, business associations (e.g., chambers of commerce, The American Bankers' Association), labor unions, professional associations (e.g., bar associations), and cooperatives of various sorts. Approximately 400,000 such organizations exist in the United States.

Public-Serving Organizations

The second category of nonprofit organizations are primarily *public-serving* in character. These are organizations that exist primarily to serve the public at large rather than primarily the members of the organization. They may do so in a variety of ways, however—providing education, sponsoring cultural activities, advocating for certain causes, aiding the poor, and many more.

Treatment in Tax Law

This distinction between primarily member-serving and primarily public-serving nonprofit organizations is far from perfect, of course. Even the member-serving organizations produce some public benefits, and the public-serving organizations often deliver benefits to their members. Yet the distinction is significant enough to find formal reflection in the law.

In particular, public-serving organizations are the only ones entitled to tax-exempt status under Section 501(c)(3) of the federal tax law. What makes this so important is that this gives such organizations a tax advantage not available to other nonprofit organizations. In particular, in addition to being exempt from taxes themselves like all nonprofit organizations, 501(c)(3) organizations are also *eligible to receive tax deductible gifts* from individuals and corporations, that is, contributions that the individuals and corporations can deduct from their own income in computing their tax liabilities. This gives the individuals and corporations a financial incentive to make contributions to these 501(c)(3) organizations because they can deduct the gifts from their taxable income. The justification for this is that the organizations are serving purposes that are public in character and that government might otherwise have to support through tax revenues.

To be eligible for this status, organizations must operate "exclusively for religious, charitable, scientif-

> *"The purpose of this chapter is to put the American nonprofit sector into perspective, to strip away some of the misperceptions and confusion, and to examine what this sector contains and how big it really is."*

ic, literary, or educational purposes."[1] The meaning of these terms is rooted in English common law, however, and is quite broad, essentially embracing organizations that promote the general welfare in any of a wide variety of ways.[2] Included, therefore, are not only agencies providing aid to the poor, but also most of the educational, cultural, social service, advocacy, self-help, health, environmental, civil rights, child welfare, and related organizations that most people have in mind when they think about the nonprofit sector. The one major exception are public-serving organizations heavily engaged in direct political action (campaigning and lobbying for legislation), for which a special section of the tax code [Section 501(c)(4)] exists.[3]

Focus on Public-Serving Organizations

Because of their essentially public character, the public-serving nonprofit organizations are the ones that most observers have in mind when they speak about the "nonprofit sector" in the United States. These are therefore the organizations that will be the principal focus of this "primer."

What is not widely appreciated, however, is that this public-serving component of the nonprofit sector contains four very different types of organizations, as shown in Figure 2.1. The first are *funding intermediaries,* that is, organizations that function chiefly to provide funds for other parts of the nonprofit sector. The second are *religious congregations,* that is, organizations that principally engage in sacramental religious observation (e.g., churches, synagogues, mosques). The third are various *service-providing organizations,* that is, organizations that provide health care, education, counseling, adoption assistance, or that advocate for particular causes. The fourth are the public-benefit

TABLE 2.1

Private Charitable Giving in the U.S., 1990, by Type of Recipient, and Purpose

Type of Recipient	Amount ($ billions)	Percent
Religious congregations	$65.8	54%
Government agencies	3.3	3
Nonprofit Service Providers	53.5	43
Education	9.1	7
Health	9.9	8
Human services	11.8	10
Arts, culture	7.9	6
Public/society benefit	4.9	4
Other	9.9	8
Total	$122.6	100%

Source: AAFRC Trust for Philanthropy, *Giving USA* (1991), government agency estimate based on data in Council for Aid to Education (1988), p. 89.

FIGURE 2.2
Nonprofit Funding Intermediaries

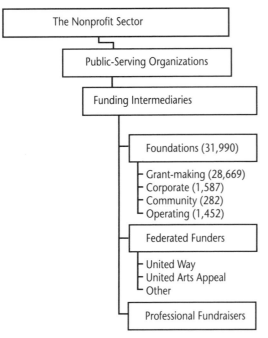

Source: Foundation data from Renz (1991), p. 2.

political action agencies noted above, which devote a significant portion of their effort to supporting particular pieces of legislation or candidates for political office. Let us look briefly at each of these types, focusing particularly on the first and third.

Funding Intermediaries

Among the public-serving nonprofit organizations in the United States, probably the best known, but least well understood, are the funding intermediaries. These are organizations whose sole, or principal, function is to channel financial support, especially private charitable support, to other nonprofit organizations.

The Scope of Private Giving

The existence of these funding intermediaries reflects the highly specialized and developed character of the U.S. nonprofit sector, which has led to the emergence of organizations that are dedicated exclusively to fundraising and fund distribution. But it also reflects the importance of private charitable giving in the United States and the scale that such giving takes. In 1990, for example, Americans contributed $123 billion to various charitable causes.[4] This represented about 2.2 percent of gross national product, considerably higher than for most other countries.[5]

Of this $123 billion, about 90 percent came from individuals and 10 percent from corporations and foundations. The largest share of this support (an estimated $66 billion or over half) went to religious organizations, mostly for sacramental religious activities. Another $3.3 billion went to public or governmental institutions of higher education. This left an estimated $53.5 billion for a wide variety of private, nonprofit service organizations (see Table 2.1).[6]

Although, as we shall see, private charitable support is by no means the only, or even the largest, source of support for American nonprofit service organizations, it is nevertheless quite important because of the role it plays in helping to ensure the sector's independence and autonomous character.

The role of the funding intermediaries is to help generate this private funding, to manage it once it is accumulated, and to make it available for use by the other organizations in the sector. Broadly speaking, as shown in Figure 2.2, three distinct types of such funding intermediaries exist: (a) foundations, (b) federated funders, and (c) professional fundraisers. Let us look briefly at each.

Foundations

Private foundations (e.g., the Ford Foundation, the Rockefeller Foundation, the Carnegie Corporation) are among the most visible components of the nonprofit sector—so much so that there is a tendency to over-state their role and confuse them with the public-serving nonprofit sector as a whole. This latter problem is particularly acute among overseas observers because the term foundation is used quite differently in most other countries. In particular there is often little distinction between foundations and other parts of the nonprofit sector elsewhere, whereas in the United States the term *foundation* is typically reserved for organizations with the more specialized function of making grants to other nonprofit organizations, typically out of the earnings from an endowment.

Altogether, as noted in Table 2.2, there were almost 32,000 foundations in the United States as of 1989, with total assets of $137.5 billion.[7] These foundations take four different forms, however.

Independent Grantmaking Foundations. The most important type of foundation by far are the so-called *independent grantmaking foundations*. These are non-profit organizations set up to administer an endowment typically left for charitable purposes by a single individual, and to distribute all or some of the earnings from that endowment to nonprofit organizations pursuing public purposes. Of the nearly 32,000 foundations in existence as of 1989, almost 29,000, or 90 percent, were independent foundations, as shown in Table 2.2. These independent foundations controlled 86 percent of all foundation assets and accounted for 75 percent of all foundation grants.

Corporate Foundations. Somewhat different from the independent foundations are the *corporate* or *company-sponsored foundations*. Unlike the independent foundations, which receive their endowments from wealthy individuals, corporate foundations receive their funds from business corporations that want to

"...although the overall scale of foundation assets seems quite large, it pales in comparison to the assets of other institutions in American society."

TABLE 2.2

U.S. Grantmaking Foundations, 1989 ($ billions)

Type	Number	Assets	Grants
Independent	28,669	$117.9	$6.0
Corporate	1,587	5.7	1.4
Community	282	6.0	0.4
Operating	1,452	7.9	0.1
Total	31,990	$137.5	$7.9

Source: Renz (1991), p. 2.

avoid the fluctuations that come from financing corporate charitable activities from current income alone. By creating corporate foundations, corporations are able to maintain more professional and stable giving programs because the foundations can receive excess funds during years of corporate prosperity to build up endowments for use when corporate profits are lower. Altogether, there were nearly 1,600 corporate foundations in 1989 and they controlled 4 percent of all foundation assets and accounted for 18 percent of all foundation grants. This excludes, of course, the amounts that corporations give to charitable purposes directly, rather than through separate foundations.

Community Foundations. A third form of foundation is the *community foundation.* Where both independent and corporate foundations receive their funds from a single source, community foundations receive them from a number of sources in a given community. The basic concept of a community foundation is that wealthy individuals in a community, rather than tying their bequests to particular organizations that may go out of business or become less relevant over time, can pool them through a community foundation and put a board of local citizens in charge of deciding what the best use of the resources might be at a given point in time. Altogether, 282 community foundations were in existence in 1989, and they accounted for 4.0 percent of all foundation assets and 5 percent of all foundation grants.

Operating Foundations. Finally, although most American foundations specialize in grantmaking, there were 1,452 foundations in 1989 that functioned both as grantmakers and operators of actual charitable programs, a pattern that is much more common overseas. These so-called *operating foundations* accounted for 6 percent of foundation assets and 1 percent of all foundation grants.

The Role of Foundations. Because of the scale of the American foundation universe, there is often a tendency to exaggerate the role that foundations play and the contribution that they make. It is, therefore, important to bear a number of crucial facts in mind in assessing the role of foundations in the American nonprofit sector.

- In the first place, although the number of American foundations is quite large, most of the foundations are quite small. In fact, as shown in Figure 2.3, the top 1 percent of all foundations—362 institutions in all—controlled 66 percent of all foundation assets as of 1989. By contrast, those with less than $10 million in assets represented 95 percent of all foundations but accounted for only

FIGURE 2.3
Distribution of Foundations and Foundation Assets, by Size Class, 1989

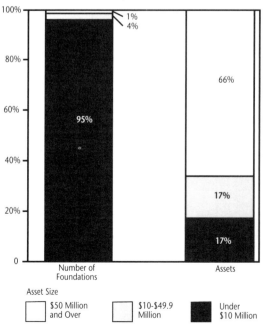

Source: Computed from Renz (1991), p. 9.

17 percent of all the assets. In other words, it is only a relative handful of foundations that account for the vast majority of foundation resources. (See Table 2.3 for a list of the top ten foundations in terms of assets.)

- In the second place, although the overall scale of foundation assets seems quite large, it pales in comparison to the assets of other institutions in American society. Thus, as Figure 2.4 shows, compared to the $137.5 billion ($.138 trillion) in foundation assets, U.S. money market funds had assets of $428 billion (3 times as much), U.S. pension funds had assets of $1.250 trillion (9 times as much), U.S. savings banks had assets of $1.520 trillion (11 times as much), U.S. nonfinancial corporations had financial assets of $1.882 trillion (14 times as much), and commercial banks had assets of $3.215 trillion (23 times as much).[8] In other words, while private foundations control significant assets, they hardly represent a major force in the American economy.

- Finally, the $7.9 billion in private foundation grants, while important, hardly represents a dominant share even of the private philanthropic support that American nonprofit organizations receive. As shown in Table 2.4, private philanthropic contributions totalled $115.9 billion in 1989. Of this total, $60.0 billion went to religious institutions and the rest for a variety of health, education, culture, social welfare, and related functions.[9] This means that the $7.9 billion in foundation grants represented only about 7 percent of all private charitable contributions and only 14 percent of all nonreligious charitable donations. And as will become clear later, private charitable contributions represent by no means the only, and not even the largest, source of income of American nonprofit organizations.

In short, the United States has an extraordinary number of private, charitable foundations. These foundations control significant assets and make important contributions to the American nonprofit sector. Nevertheless, it would be wrong to exaggerate the role that these organizations play. They are by no means the dominant source of charitable donations and represent an even smaller share of the overall income of American nonprofits.

Federated Funders

Beyond the foundations, a second broad group of "funding intermediaries" in the American nonprofit sector are so-called federated funders. These organizations that collect private donations on behalf of a

TABLE 2.3
Ten Largest U.S. Foundations, 1989

Name	Assets ($ billions)
Ford Foundation	$5.8
J. Paul Getty Trust	4.5
W.K. Kellogg Foundation	4.2
Lilly Endowment Inc.	3.4
The Pew Charitable Trusts	3.3
MacArthur Foundation	3.2
Johnson Foundation	2.6
The Rockefeller Foundation	2.1
Andrew W. Mellon Foundation	1.8
The Kresge Foundation	1.3
Total	$32.2

Souce: Renz (1991), p. 5.

FIGURE 2.4
Financial Assets, U.S. Institutions, 1989

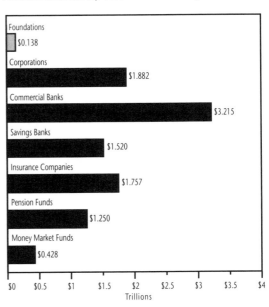

Source: *Statistical Abstract of the United States, 1991*, Table 797, p. 497.

number of service organizations. Examples here would be the United Jewish Appeal, the Lutheran social services network, the Cancer Society, federated arts appeals, and the like.

Perhaps the most important of these federated funding organizations, however, is the *United Way*. United Way is a network of some 2,300 local "community chests" that raise funds from individuals on behalf of a number of local social service agencies. What is distinctive about the United Way system, however, is its use of a particular mode of fundraising, namely, "workplace solicitation." This essentially involves a direct charitable appeal to workers in their workplace coupled with a system allowing employers to deduct the pledged contributions made by their employees automatically from the employees' paychecks each pay period. In order to ensure employer support, United Way has typically involved the corporate community actively in the organization of each year's United Way "campaign," and has historically restricted the distribution of the proceeds of the campaign to a set of approved United Way "member agencies." This latter feature has come under increasing attack in recent years, however, with the result that many local United Ways have established "donor option" plans, which permit donors to designate which agencies will receive their contributions.

Because of its obvious efficiencies, United Way's workplace campaigns have been quite effective, so much so that many other federated fundraising organizations have sought to break the monopoly that United Way has long had on the workplace as a solicitation site.[10] In 1990, for example, local United Ways throughout the United Sates collected a total of $3.1 billion in contributions.[11] While this is quite significant, it represented only about 3 percent of all private

TABLE 2.4

Sources of Private Giving in the United States, 1989 ($ billions)

Source	Total		Excluding Religion	
	Amount	%	Amount	%
Individuals	$96.8	83%	$36.8	6%
Foundations	7.9	7	7.9	14
Corporations*	4.2	4	4.2	8
Bequests	7.0	6	7.0	12
Total	$115.9	100%	$55.9	100%

*Excludes corporate foundations.
Source: Computed from data in *Giving USA* (1991), pp. 8-9; Renz (1991), p. 2; and Hodgkinson and Weitzman (1992), p. 148. See footnote 9.

charitable donations to American nonprofit organizations, or about 40 percent as much as is provided by foundations. In the human service field in which it focuses, United Way provides closer to 25 percent of all the charitable support, but it is still important to remember that charitable support is just one of the sources of nonprofit income, and by no means the largest source.

Recent years have witnessed an expansion of the role of federated fundraising, even as individual nonprofit organizations have increased their direct appeals as well. Federated fundraising minimizes costs, especially for direct mail and related types of campaigning, but it also creates serious challenges in figuring out how to distribute the proceeds of federated campaigns and how to create donor identification with the causes and agencies being supported.

Professional Fundraisers

A final group of financial intermediaries of great importance to the nonprofit sector are professional fundraisers, the individuals and firms professionally involved in raising private contributions on behalf of private, nonprofit organizations. Larger nonprofit organizations typically employ one or more professional fundraisers on their regular staffs, and the typical large university or cultural institution may have a "development office" that employs 20 or 25 fundraisers. These professional fundraisers have their own professional association, the National Society of Fund-Raising Executives (NSFRE), as well as extensive networks of workshops and training courses. As of 1991, NSFRE had 11,873 members throughout the United States.[12] In addition, a significant number of for-profit fundraising firms exist. For example, the American Association of Fund-Raising Counsel, Inc. represents approximately 35 of these firms. Such firms work on retainers from nonprofit organizations to manage fundraising campaigns.

Summary

In short, the American nonprofit sector contains a significant number of major institutions whose principal function is to serve as financial intermediaries, generating philanthropic contributions from the public, managing philanthropic asset pools, and transferring the resulting proceeds of both activities to other nonprofit organizations for their use. The existence of these organizations is at once a reflection of the maturity and specialization of the American nonprofit sector and of the premium that is placed on private, charitable support for it. But it can also be a source of confusion for those unacquainted with this class of organization.

"Foundation grants represented only about 7 percent of all private charitable contributions...and private charitable contributions represent by no means the only, or even largest, source of income of American nonprofit organizations."

Religious Congregations

In addition to the funding intermediaries, a second broad class of public-serving nonprofit organizations are the numerous sacramental religious organizations. Included here are the close to 350,000 religious congregations—churches, mosques, synagogues, and other places of worship—as well as an assortment of conventions of churches, religious orders, apostolic groups, and religious auxiliaries.[13]

The placement of these religious organizations in the primarily "public-serving" category is, of course, open to question. Although they often engage in a variety of service functions, religious congregations really exist primarily to serve the needs of their members rather than the public more generally. They are grouped in the public-serving category here because of the favored position they occupy in American law: They are the only organizations that are *automatically* entitled to tax exemption under Section 501(c)(3) of the tax code, and thus to the receipt of tax deductible donations, without even having to file an application for formal recognition from the Internal Revenue Service. They are also exempt from the reporting requirements that the law places on all other types of 501(c)(3) organizations.

"Because the power to tax is the power to destroy, it is felt that to require religious congregations to secure approval from government to be incorporated or exempted from taxation would be to give government too much potential control over them."

This favored position reflects the strong separation of church and state built into the American constitution.[14] Because the power to tax is the power to destroy, it is felt that to require religious congregations to secure approval from government to be incorporated or exempted from taxation would be to give government too much potential control over them. A self-declared religious congregation is therefore automatically treated as a 501(c)(3) organization exempt from taxes and eligible to receive tax-deductible gifts.

What constitutes a religious congregation or church for this purpose is open to dispute, however. Federal authorities have historically been loath to define the term very precisely in view of the First Amendment's prohibitions on any laws regarding the establishment of religion or the free exercise thereof. But the appearance of various self-styled religious organizations that turn out to be fronts for nonexempt activities has led the courts and the Internal Revenue Service to be somewhat more precise. Thus, churches and religious organizations are expected, among other things, to have some recognized creed or form of worship, to be sacerdotal in character, to have regular religious services, and to operate, like other 501(c)(3) organizations, for other than private gain.[15]

Service Providers

We come now to what in many respects is the heart of the public-serving nonprofit sector: the broad assortment of organizations that are neither funding inter-mediaries nor sacramental religious congregations but rather service- providing organizations. Included are providers of health services, education, day care, adoption services, counseling, community organization, employment and training, arts, culture, music, theater, and hundreds of others. Also included, however, are research institutes, advocacy organizations seeking to promote particular causes or call attention to social and economic ills, community-based organizations, and organizations involved in overseas relief and development.

To make sense of this welter of organizations, it is useful to group them into five basic fields:[16]

- *health care*, including hospitals, clinics, nursing and personal care facilities, home health care centers, and specialty facilities (e.g., kidney dialysis units);
- *education,* including elementary and secondary education, higher education, libraries, vocational schools, noncommercial research institutes, and related educational services;
- *social and legal services*, including individual and family social services, job training and vocational rehabilitation services, residential care, day care, and legal aid services;
- *civic and social*, including advocacy organizations, civil rights organizations, neighborhood based organizations; and
- *arts and culture*, including bands, orchestras, theater groups, museums, art galleries, and botanical and zoological gardens.

Service versus Action Organizations

Legally, two broad classes of these service organizations exist. The principal distinction between these two classes is the extent to which they engage in active legislative lobbying. The first class includes organizations that are primarily service providers and that can engage in advocacy and public education activities only as a subsidiary activity. Such organizations are recognized as tax exempt under Section 501(c)(3) of the tax code as "charitable" organizations. The second class is composed of organizations that are *primarily* engaged in advocacy, lobbying, and other legislative activity. Such organizations must register under Section 501(c)(4) of the tax code as "social welfare organizations." As such, they are not eligible to receive tax deductible gifts from corporations or the general public.

Because of this restriction, many 501(c)(3) organizations, restricted from engaging "substantially" in lobbying activities themselves, organize (c)(4) "politi-

FIGURE 2.5
Scope of U.S. Nonprofit Public-Benefit Service Sector*

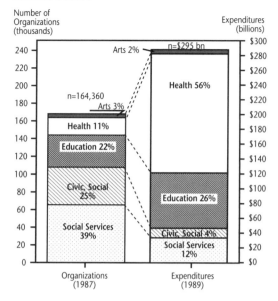

Source: U.S. Census Bureau (1991); U.S. Department of Education (1991); Hodgkinson and Weizman (1992).
*Includes only organizations with one paid employee.

"...in addition to their social value, nonprofit organizations are also a major economic force."

cal action" affiliates to handle their lobbying activities for them without jeopardizing the tax deductible status for the rest of the organization's operations. For purposes of our discussion here, however, we will treat both the primarily service organizations and the primarily "action" organizations as service providers.

Numbers of Organizations

Solid data on the scope of this nonprofit service sector, or of its constituent parts, are difficult to piece together and sensitive to differences in record-keeping (e.g., some organizations treat their branches as separate organizations and others as integral parts of a single parent organization; many organizations carry out a multitude of activities and cannot easily be classified in one category). Based on the available data, however, it appears that there were approximately 360,000 active nonprofit, public-benefit service organizations as of 1987, the latest date for which data are available.[17] Of these, more detailed information is available on those with at least one paid employee. As of 1987, there were 164,360 such organizations.[18]

As shown in Figure 2.5, these organizations are not distributed evenly among the various service fields. Rather:

- The *social service agencies* are the most numerous. Close to 40 percent of nonprofit service organizations fall into this category.

- The next largest group are the *civic and social organizations*, which includes neighborhood associations, advocacy organizations, civil rights organizations and the like. Twenty-five percent of nonprofit service organizations take this form.

- Another 22 percent of the nonprofit service organizations are *educational institutions*, including private elementary and secondary schools as well as private universities and colleges.

- *Health organizations*, including hospitals, nursing homes, and clinics, comprise 11 percent of the organizations.

- The smallest component of the nonprofit service sector is the *arts and culture component*, which includes symphonies, art galleries, theaters, zoos, botanical gardens, and other cultural institutions. Together, these cultural organizations represent 3 percent of the nonprofit organizations.

Expenditures: A Major Economic Force

Because of the growth of government spending in recent decades and the prominence given to government policies, it is widely believed that this nonprofit service sector has shrunk into insignificance. Yet nothing could be further from the truth. To the contrary, in addition to their social value, nonprofit organizations are also a major economic force. In particular, these nonprofit public-benefit service organizations had expenditures in 1989 of approximately $295 billion, or almost 6 percent of the country's gross national product.[19] In many local areas, in fact, the expenditures of the nonprofit sector easily outdistance those of local government. For example, a recent study of the nonprofit sector in Baltimore, Maryland, revealed that nonprofit expenditures in this metropolitan area exceeded the total expenditures of the city of Baltimore and the five surrounding counties.[20]

The distribution of expenditures differs widely, however, from the distribution of organizations. In particular, as Figure 2.5 also shows:

- *Health dominance.* The health subsector, composed in part of huge hospital complexes, accounts for the lion's share of the sector's total resources even though it comprises a relatively small proportion of the organizations. In particular, with 11 percent of the organizations the health subsector accounts for 56 percent of all nonprofit service-organization expenditures.

- *Significant education presence.* The education subsector accounted for another 26 percent of the expenditures. Health and education organizations alone thus control over 80 percent of the sector's expenditures.

- *Balance of the sector.* By contrast, the social service, civic and social, and arts organizations, which represent altogether two out of every three (66 percent) of the organizations, accounted for less than one out of every five (18 percent) of the expenditure dollars.

Quite clearly, this is a sector with a great deal of diversity in the size of its component organizations.

Where Do Nonprofit Service Agencies Get Their Funds?

Compared to their $295 billion in operating expenditures, America's nonprofit, public-benefit service organizations had revenues in 1989 of approximately $343 billion.[21] Included in the revenue figure are sums that were spent for nonoperating expenses such as capital equipment and buildings, as well as income in excess of amounts spent.

Where did these resources come from? What are the major sources of nonprofit revenues?

Unfortunately, there is a great deal of misunderstanding about the answer to this question. One common belief has been that large charitable foundations provide most of the income of America's nonprofit sector. Another is that charitable contributions as a

"...a recent study of the nonprofit sector in Baltimore, Maryland, revealed that nonprofit expenditures in this metropolitan area exceeded the total expenditures of the city of Baltimore and the five surrounding counties."

"Important as private giving is to the vitality and independence of the nonprofit sector, it is hardly the largest source of nonprofit service-organization revenue. Rather, most of the income of this sector comes from fees and service charges, with government a close second."

whole, including individual and corporate gifts as well as foundation grants, account for the bulk of nonprofit service-organization income.

As we saw earlier in this chapter, however, private foundations account for only 7 percent of the private charitable contributions that are given in the United States. And total charitable contributions amounted to only $53 billion in income to nonprofit service organizations in 1989, $64 billion if estimated indirect contributions through churches are included.[22] This compares to total revenues of $343 billion. In other words, private giving from all sources constituted only 15 percent of nonprofit income, 18 percent if estimated contributions through churches are included. Clearly, important as private charitable support may be to the independence of the nonprofit sector, it hardly comprises the major source of income.

What, then, are the major sources of income? The answer to this question may be found in Figure 2.6. As this figure shows:

- *Fees, service charges, and other commercial income.* The major source of support of America's nonprofit, public-benefit, service organizations are fees, service charges, and other commercial income. Included here are college tuition payments, charges for hospital care not covered by government health insurance, other direct payments for services, and income from investments and sales of products. This source alone accounts for over half of all nonprofit service-organization revenues.

- *Government.* The second most important source of income of America's nonprofit, public-benefit, service organizations is government. Government grants, contracts, and reimbursements account for 31 percent of nonprofit service-organization income. This reflects a widespread pattern of partnership between government and the nonprofit sector in carrying out public purposes, from the delivery of health care to the provision of education.[23]

- *Private giving.* The 18 percent of total income that nonprofits receive from private giving makes this only the third largest source of nonprofit service-organization income.

Variations by Subsector

There are important differences in the revenue structure of different components of the nonprofit sector, however. As shown in Figure 2.7:

- *Fee dominance in health and education.* The health and education portions of the nonprofit service sector, which are by far the largest, receive disproportionate shares of their income from fees, service

FIGURE 2.6
Sources of Nonprofit Public Benefit Organization Income, 1989

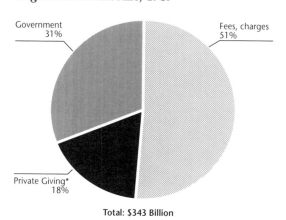

Total: $343 Billion

Source: Compiled from data in Hodgkinson and Weitzman (1992), p. 147.
*Includes estimated indirect giving through churches.

charges, and other commercial income (55 and 63 percent, respectively).

- *Government dominance in social services and civic.* Social and legal service and civic and social organizations, by contrast, receive disproportionately large portions of their income from government (42 and 41 percent, respectively). Private giving also plays a significant role in the financing of these organizations, but still lags behind government.

- *Private dominance in culture.* Of all the types of nonprofit organizations, only one—arts and culture—receives the preponderance of its income from private charitable sources. Even this is potentially misleading, however, because a significant share of the private contributions to nonprofit culture and arts organizations takes the form of contributed art works or other capital items (buildings, equipment). If we exclude such nonoperating income and focus only on operating support, the funding structure of arts organizations comes to resemble that for health and education organizations, with private giving representing closer to 31 percent of the total.

Volunteer Time

In addition to the cash income they receive, nonprofit service organizations also have access to the services of numerous volunteers. Recent estimates indicate that 98 million Americans volunteered an average of 4 hours per week to various charitable and other organizations in 1989, and public-serving nonprofit service organizations are the beneficiaries of a significant portion of this.[24] In fact, the volunteer labor available to these organizations translates into the equivalent of almost three million full-time employees. If these

"The volunteer labor available to nonprofit, public-benefit, service organizations translates into the equivalent of almost three million full-time employees a year."

FIGURE 2.7
Sources of Nonprofit Organization Revenue, by Type of Agency, 1989

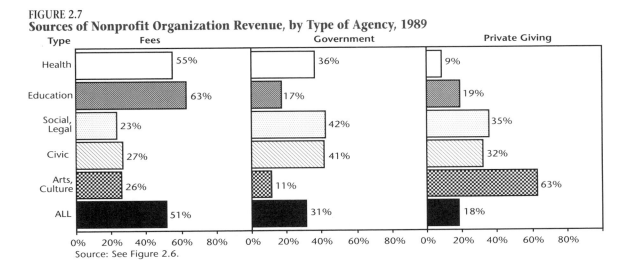

Source: See Figure 2.6.

organizations had to hire such employees, the cost would be nearly $52 billion. Therefore, it is possible to consider this volunteer time as contributing another $52 billion to the revenues of the public-benefit service sector, of which nearly half goes to social services and civic organizations, and nearly the other half to health, education, and arts organizations.[25] Including the assigned value of volunteers thus brings the total revenue of these organizations to $395 billion in 1989.

Comparison to Other Countries

Although solid comparative data on the scope of the nonprofit sector in other countries is not available, preliminary estimates put the size elsewhere proportionately much lower than in the United States. In the United Kingdom, for example, the expenditures of the equivalent organizations is approximately only half as large as in the United States (2.5 percent of gross national product vs. 6 percent).

Summary

Three principal conclusions flow from this overview of the American nonprofit sector:

(1) **The nonprofit sector is composed of many different types of organizations.** Some of these are essentially member-serving organizations, and others are primarily public-serving. Among the public-serving organizations, a great deal of specialization also exists. Some organizations are essentially funding intermediaries, others are places of sacramental religious worship, and others provide the services for which the sector is best known.

(2) **The nonprofit sector is much larger than is commonly believed.** America's nonprofit, public-benefit service organizations had operating expenditures in 1989 that were the equivalent of 6 percent of the gross national product. In many locales, the expenditures of the nonprofit sector outdistance those of all local governments.

(3) **Private giving comprises a much smaller share of the income of the nonprofit sector than is commonly recognized.** Important as private giving is to the vitality and independence of the nonprofit sector, it is hardly the largest source of nonprofit service-organization revenue. Rather, most of the income of this sector comes from fees and service charges, with government a close second.

ENDNOTES

1. The formal language of the law is somewhat more complex than this. Section 501(c)(3) status is available for: "Corporations, and any community chest, fund or foundation, organized and operated exclusively for religious, charitable, scientific, testing for public safety, literary, or educational purposes, or to foster national or international amateur sports competition (but only if no part of its activities involve the provision of athletic facilities or equipment), or for the prevention of cruelty to children or animals."

2. The English Statute of Charitable Uses of 1601, which is the basis of the legal definition of the term *charitable,* specifically included the following activities within the term charitable: "...relief of aged, impotent, and poor people;...maintenance of sick and maimed soldiers and mariners; schools for learning, free schools, and scholars in universities; repair of bridges, ports, havens, causeways, churches, seabanks, and highways;...education and preferment of orphans;...relief, stock or maintenance of house of correction;...marriages of poor maids; supportation, aid, and help of young tradesmen, handicraftsmen and persons decayed; relief or redemption of prisoners or captives; aid or ease of any poor inhabitants concerning payments of fifteens, setting out of soldiers and other taxes." For further detail, see: Bruce R. Hopkins, *The Law of Tax-Exempt Organizations*, 5th edition. (New York: John Wiley & Sons, 1987), pp. 55-71.

3. The reason for this is that Section 501(c)(3) of the Internal Revenue Code law puts certain restrictions on the extent to which organizations can engage in "lobbying" activities, that is, activities intended to affect the passage or defeat of legislation. Organizations that intend to devote a substantial part of their activities to influencing legislation must seek tax-exempt status under Section 501(c)(4) of the Internal Revenue Code, which is reserved for "civic leagues or organizations not organized for profit but operated exclusively for the promotion of social welfare..." Like "charitable" organizations exempted under section 501(c)(3), the "welfare organizations" granted exemption under section 501(c)(4) must be primarily public-serving and not member-serving in orientation, but they are allowed to be more action-oriented in political terms. In return, however, they cannot receive tax deductible gifts. We have therefore depicted these organizations in Figure 2.1 in a special category tied to the others by a dotted line. For more detail on the similarities and differences between 501(c)(3) and 501(c)(4) organizations, see Hopkins (1987), pp. 311-314.

4. AAFRC Trust for Philanthropy, *Giving USA* ed. by Nathan Weber (New York: AAFRC Trust for Philanthropy, Inc., 1991), p. 8.

5. Comparable data for the United Kingdom, for example, reveals that private giving represents only about 1.4 percent of gross domestic product. Charities Aid Foundation, *Charity Trends*. 13th edition. (London: Charities

Aid Foundation, 1990), p. 10.

6. This estimate is based on data developed by the American Association of Fundraising Counsel (AAFRC) in *Giving USA*, the most comprehensive source of data on private charitable giving in the United States. However, because of the absence of solid data on religious giving, AAFRC treats religion as a residual category in its data and allocates to it all giving that cannot be reliably allocated to any other sector. An alternative treatment is suggested in an estimate of the scale of the nonprofit sector produced regularly by Independent Sector, the umbrella group representing the nonprofit sector in the United States. In Independent Sector's *Dimensions of the Independent Sector*, analysts Virginia Hodgkinson and Murray Weitzman assume that 25 percent of all the religious giving they identify is reallocated to non-sacramental religious activities such as health and education. The result is a much smaller estimate of giving for religious purposes and a much larger estimate of giving for other nonprofit activities, especially if the "unallocated" portion is attributed wholly to the latter category. Thus, while AAFRC estimated giving to religion at $62.5 billion in 1989, Independent Sector estimated it at only $48.5 billion, and left $17.7 billion in an "unallocated" category. It then allocated $11.5 billion of the private giving to religious organizations to nonreligious purposes, yielding an estimate of giving to religion of only $37.0 billion, or only 60 percent of the AAFRC figure. As will be noted more fully below (endnote 20), we consider the Independent Sector estimate of giving to religion to be understated and think a more reasonable approach is to allocate the "unallocated" portion identified by Independent Sector between religion and other charities roughly in proportion to the share of individual giving that survey data indicate goes to each. For further detail, see: *Giving USA* (1991), pp. 16, 216; Virginia A. Hodgkinson and Murray S. Weitzman, *Dimensions of the Independent Sector*, 3rd edition (Washington, DC: Independent Sector, 1989), pp. 202-203 [cited hereafter as Hodgkinson and Weitzman (1989)]; and Virginia A. Hodgkinson, Murray S. Weitzman, Christopher M. Toppe, and Stephen M. Noga. *Nonprofit Almanac 1992-1993: Dimensions of the Independent Sector* (San Francisco, CA: Jossey-Bass Publishers, Inc., 1992), p. 148 [cited hereafter as Hodgkinson, Weitzman, et. al. (1992)].

7. Loren Renz, *Foundation Giving*, 1991 edition. (New York: The Foundation Center, 1991), p. 2. All data on foundations here comes from this source.

8. U.S. Bureau of the Census, *Statistical Abstract of the United States, 1991,* 111th edition (Washington, DC: U.S. Government Printing Office, 1991), p. 497.

9. The estimate of religious giving here is based on Independent Sector data adjusted as noted in endnote 6, above. In particular, 65 percent of the $17.7 billion in "unallocated" private giving identified by Independent Sector is attributed to religion. The 65 percent figure represents the share of total *individual* giving that goes to religious organizations according to a population survey

conducted by the Gallup organization for Independent Sector. See: Virginia Hodgkinson and Murray Weitzman, *Giving and Volunteering in the United States: Findings from a National Survey*, 1990 edition (Washington, DC: Independent Sector, 1990), p. 26; Hodgkinson, Weitzman, et. al. (1992), p. 148.

10. During the Carter Administration, several alternative funds, such as the Black United Fund and the United Health Appeal, secured permission to solicit contributions in the federal workplace. This was later revoked by the Reagan Administration, provoking a legal battle that has ended with a broadening of the access to the federal workplace and a greater willingness of the United Way to accept the donor option approach. For this and other features of United Way, see: Eleanor Brilliant, *The United Way: Dilemmas of Organized Charity* (New York: Columbia University Press, 1991).

11. *Giving USA* (1991), p. 155.

12. William Harrison, Librarian, NSFRE, personal interview, July 20, 1991.

13. *Yearbook of American and Canadian Churches* (New York: National Council of the Churches of Christ in the United States, 1990); *Statistical Abstract of the United States* (Washington: U.S. Government Printing Office, 1990), p. 50. For a discussion of the definitions of these various types of religious organizations, see: Hopkins (1987), pp. 198-209. The 350,000 religious congregations included here do not include the religiously affiliated service organizations, such as the agencies that are part of the Catholic Charities network or the Lutheran Social Services network. These agencies are included among the service agencies discussed later.

14. The First Amendment to the U.S. Constitution declares, "Congress shall make no law respecting an establishment of religion, or prohibiting the free exercise thereof."

15. Organizations that are church-related but that would be eligible for tax-exempt 501(c)(3) status for other than religious reasons (e.g., church-affiliated educational organizations, hospitals, orphanages, old-age homes) are required to be recognized under these other provisions and are not treated as churches. Typically such organizations must therefore secure separate tax-exempt status and are not covered by the exemption accorded the church qua church. Reflecting this, we do not treat them here as religious congregations, but rather as service organizations. On the treatment of churches and church-related charitable organizations, see: Hopkins (1987), p. 646.

16. This classification follows U.S. Census of Service Industry usage and is embraced here for convenience sake. The chapters in Part II of this volume separate out legal aid from other social services and group it with political action and international aid agencies.

17. This estimate was developed by subtracting from the 560,588 organizations registered as 501(c)(3) or 501(c)(4) organizations on the Internal Revenue Service's Master File of Tax-Exempt Organizations the approximately

half of all churches that choose to register with the Internal Revenue Service even though they are not required to, and the approximately 30,000 private foundations. This figure is still very likely a gross underestimate of the scale of the nonprofit, public-benefit service sector because organizations with gross revenues of less than $5,000 are not required to file with the Internal Revenue Service. IRS data are from U.S. Internal Revenue Service, *Annual Report of the Director* (1988).

18. Included here are 135,931 organizations identified by the U.S. Census Bureau in its 1987 Census of Service Industries in the categories that meet our definition of public-benefit service organizations, and 28,429 schools, colleges, and universities identified in the *Digest of Education Statistics*. Supplementation of the census data is necessary because the census did not cover schools and colleges. Deleted from the census data are certain member-serving organizations that do not meet our definition. For further information, see: U.S. Census Bureau, *1987 Census of Service Industries* (Washington: U.S. Government Printing Office, Nov. 1989), Table 1B, p. US-13; and U.S. Department of Education, National Center for Education Statistics, *Digest of Education Statistics*, 1990, Tables 53 and 217, pp. 68 and 229.

19. Based on data in Hodgkinson, Weitzman, et al. (1992), Table 4.2, p. 147. Excludes religious organizations and foundations.

20. Lester M. Salamon, David Altschuler, and Jaana Myllyluoma, *More Than Just Charity: The Baltimore Nonprofit Sector in a Time of Change* (Baltimore: The Johns Hopkins Institute for Policy Studies, 1990), p. 9.

21. Computed from estimates developed in Hodgkinson, Weitzman, et al. (1992).

22. This assumes that 25 percent of all religious contributions find their way to non-sacramental service organizations. Hodgkinson, Weitzman, et al. (1992), p.147.

23. For more detail on this government-nonprofit financial link, see Chapter 4.

24. Hodgkinson and Weitzman, *Giving and Volunteering* (1990), p. 2.

25. This estimate values the volunteer contribution to these organizations as equivalent to the average gross hourly earnings plus 12 percent for fringe benefits. Hodgkinson, Weitzman, et al. (1992).

CHAPTER THREE

The Government Role in America's Mixed Economy of Welfare

Important as the nonprofit sector is to American society and the American social welfare system, it hardly operates in a vacuum. Nor does it have a monopoly on providing for public needs. To the contrary, one of the signal developments of the past half century of American life has been the expansion of governmental social welfare activity, so much so that some observers have feared that government may have displaced the nonprofit sector altogether.

As we have seen, this fear has been largely unwarranted. The presumed conflict between an activist government and a vibrant nonprofit sector has not really materialized in the American setting. Although tensions clearly exist, a widespread partnership has also developed between the two sectors, and with for-profit businesses as well, a "mixed economy" of welfare in which public and private, nonprofit and for profit, action are mixed in often complex and confusing ways[1]. Thus:

- Nonprofit organizations help to identify problems and mobilize pressure on government to respond.

- Government establishes programs and raises resources and then turns to both nonprofit and for-profit organizations to deliver the services.

- Private households purchase welfare services on their own from both nonprofit and for-profit providers.

The purpose of this chapter is to outline the basic scope and structure of governmental involvement in this "mixed economy" of social welfare and to assess how valid the claim is that government has surpassed the nonprofit sector in the provision of social welfare services.

To do so, the discussion here falls into two major sections. The first provides an overview of govern-

"In 1989, federal, state, and local governments in the United States spent a total of $956 billion—19 percent of the U.S. gross national product and over half of all government spending—on 'social welfare' activities."

"...far from being overshadowed by government, the nonprofit sector in the United States is almost as large in the fields where both are actively involved. In fact, the nonprofit sector is a more significant provider than either state and local governments or the federal government."

ment social welfare spending, the distribution of this spending between federal and state and local governments, and the relationship between the levels of such spending in the United States and that in other countries. Against this backdrop, we then zero in on those areas where nonprofit organizations are involved and compare the level of government involvement in these areas with the levels of nonprofit activity in the same fields.

What emerges from this analysis are four basic conclusions:

- First, government social welfare spending is quite extensive in the United States.

- Second, despite the expansion of federal government activity, state and local governments still play a significant role in many fields.

- Third, government social welfare spending in the United States, however significant, is still well below comparable levels in most of the other advanced industrial societies.

- Fourth, far from being overshadowed by government, the nonprofit sector in the United States is almost as large in the fields where both are actively involved.

The remainder of this chapter examines the bases for these conclusions.

The Government Role: Basic Parameters

Overview

In 1989, the latest year for which data are available, federal, state, and local governments in the United States spent a total of $956 billion on "social welfare services." Included here are old-age pensions, unemployment insurance, veterans benefits, education, health care, welfare aid for the poor, nutrition assistance, day care, social services, housing, and related services.[2] This represented approximately 19 percent of the total U.S. gross national product and just over half (53 percent) of all government spending—federal, state, and local.

As noted in Figure 3.1:

- The largest portion (41 percent) of this social welfare spending went for *social security, veterans benefits (excluding health and education), and other social insurance and pension benefits.* Included here is the federal social security program, which provides pension benefits to retired workers; unemployment insurance, which provides cash payments to unemployed persons in covered occupations for a limited period following loss of a job; disability payments to persons injured while working; and

FIGURE 3.1
Government Spending on Social Welfare in the U.S., 1989

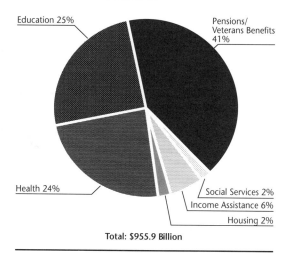

Total: $955.9 Billion

Source: Compiled from data in Bixby (November 1991).

pension payments to injured war veterans. These benefits are typically conditioned only on past work or military experience and are not income related.[3]

- About one-fourth (25 percent) of government social welfare spending goes for *education*, of which the lion's share (19 percent) is for elementary and secondary education and 6 percent for higher education.

- Nearly another quarter (24 percent) of government social welfare spending goes for *health* benefits. This included payments for Medicare, the federal health program providing health insurance for the elderly; and for Medicaid, a joint federal-state program providing reimbursement to hospitals and nursing homes for health services to the poor.

- This left only 10 percent to be split among a variety of *income assistance or "welfare" programs, housing aid, and a smorgasbord of child nutrition, vocational rehabilitation, institutional care, and related social services.* Included here is the Aid to Families with Dependent Children Program, the basic cash assistance program for the poor; Food Stamps, which provides food assistance to the needy; public housing; and a variety of employment assistance and social service programs.

Quite clearly, the basic, universal, or non-needs-tested, assistance programs for the elderly and for education dominate the government role in the social welfare field, and the assistance targeted particularly on the poor is far more limited.

Federal versus State and Local Roles

Much of the impetus for the growth of government social welfare spending over the past four or five decades has come from the national level, giving rise to the common assumption that state and local involvement, once dominant, has now effectively disappeared. In fact, however, state and local governments retain a substantial role in financing, as well as delivering, government social welfare services in the United States. In particular:

- Of the $956 billion in government social welfare spending in 1989, only 59 percent came from the federal government. The remaining 41 percent came from state and local governments.

- As shown in Figure 3.2, federal spending dominates in the areas of pensions (Social Security and veterans' payments), and housing aid.

- State and local governments have the decidedly dominant role in education, especially elementary and secondary education.

FIGURE 3.2
Federal vs. State/Local Spending on Social Welfare, 1989

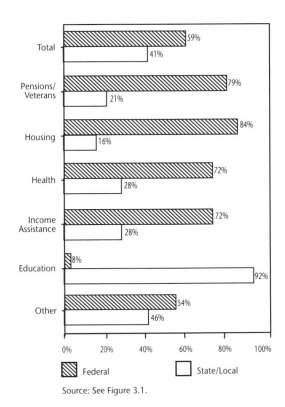

Source: See Figure 3.1.

"...the expansion of federal social welfare activity has by no means displaced the state and local governments....To the contrary, these governments retain a vital role...."

- In addition, state and local governments account for nearly half of the support for a broad range of other social service activities.
- Even in the costly health care and income assistance areas, the states provide slightly over a quarter of all the support. This reflects state and local financing of much of public health and the "matching" requirements built into the federal Medicaid and AFDC programs.
- Beyond their financing role, moreover, state and local governments frequently play a major role in the implementation of even the federally financed activity. Thus, the federal Medicaid and AFDC programs are essentially administered by state and local governments. State and local governments also operate the federal Social Service Block Grant and Community Development Block Grant programs.

In short, the expansion of federal social welfare activity has by no means displaced the state and local governments. To the contrary, federal aid has helped to expand the role of state and local governments, and these governments retain a vital role both in the financing and delivery of social welfare services.

Comparison to Other Countries

While the government role in social welfare provision is quite extensive in the United States, it still lags far behind that in most of the other developed countries of the world. Compared to the 19 percent of gross national product that government social welfare spending represents in the United States, most of the developed nations of Europe devote 30 percent or more of their gross national products to government-funded social welfare activities (Figure 3.3).[4] This reflects the different conceptions about public versus individual responsibility for social welfare between the United States and Europe. What is treated as a public responsibility in Europe is often considered a private responsibility, to be financed out of private earnings, in the United States. Significantly, moreover, although the United States boasts a larger private nonprofit sector than do almost all of these other countries, the difference does not come close to evening out the disparities in government social welfare spending. At most, the inclusion of the nonprofit sector would narrow the disparity in the share of gross national product devoted to social welfare purposes between the United States and these other advanced industrial countries by only 2 percent, leaving a gap of anywhere from 8 percent to 15 percent of gross national product—a quite substantial difference.[5]

"...compared to the 19 percent of gross national product that the United States devotes to government-funded social welfare spending, most of the developed nations of Europe devote 30 percent or more."

FIGURE 3.3
Government Social Welfare Spending as a Share of G.D.P., U.S. vs. W. Europe

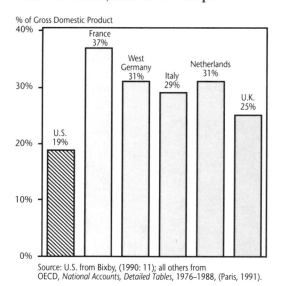

Source: U.S. from Bixby, (1990: 11); all others from OECD, *National Accounts, Detailed Tables*, 1976–1988, (Paris, 1991).

Government versus the Nonprofit Sector

At first glance, the $956 billion in government social welfare spending does indeed appear to overshadow by a substantial margin the $295 billion in nonprofit expenditures as of 1989, not to mention the $53.5 billion in private charitable support to nonprofit service providers.

For purposes of comparing the scale of government activity to the scale of nonprofit activity, however, it is not appropriate to include all of what is here referred to as "social welfare expenditures." The nonprofit sector is not, for example, involved in providing pensions or veterans' benefits, and its involvement in elementary and secondary education is quite limited, as will be detailed more fully below. With these two major components excluded, we are left with $382 billion in government spending on welfare services that are similar to those provided by the nonprofit sector, as shown in Figure 3.4.

Of this $382 billion, $138 billion represents state and local government spending and $244 billion represents federal spending.

What this means is that for every five dollars of government spending in the fields where government and the nonprofit sector are both involved, nonprofit organizations spend almost four dollars. (see Figure 3.5). What is more, nonprofit expenditures in these fields outdistance those of either the federal government, or state and local governments, taken separately. To be sure, a significant share of the nonprofit expenditures come from government support, but the key point is that the scale of nonprofit activity, even measured solely in monetary terms, is almost as large as government activity as a whole, more than twice as large as the state and local government role alone, and 20 percent larger than the federal role alone! These disparities would widen further, moreover, if we were to include the $52 billion worth of volunteer labor that the nonprofit sector also brings into the field.

Summary

In short:

(1) **Government is thus a major presence in the social welfare field in the United States. In fact over half of all government spending in the United States goes for social welfare purposes, broadly conceived.**

(2) **Although the growth of federal involvement has played a critical part in creating this government presence, state and local governments have played an important part as well and retain a sig-**

FIGURE 3.4
Major Components of Government Social Welfare Spending, 1989

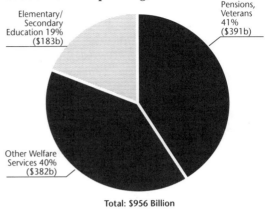

Total: $956 Billion

Source: See Figure 3.1.

FIGURE 3.5
Spending on Social Welfare:* Government vs. Private Nonprofit Organizations, 1989

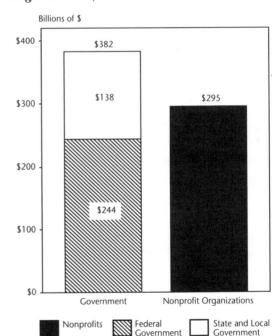

*Excludes old age pensions, veterans pensions, and public elementary and secondary education.
Source: Government figures from Bixby (1990), pp. 18–21; nonprofit figures from Hodgkinson, Weitzman et. al. (1992), p. 147.

nificant role. In fact, fully 40 percent of all government social welfare spending originates at the state and local government level, and state and local governments play an even broader role in operating programs financed in part with federal resources.

(3) Although sizable, the level of government social welfare spending in the United States, when measured as a share of gross national product, lags significantly behind that in most other advanced industrial societies. In part this reflects the greater reliance Americans place on private charity and the nonprofit sector. But in even greater part it probably reflects the greater reliance Americans place on private purchase of social welfare services.

(4) Finally, and most significantly for our purposes here, important as the government role in providing for social welfare is, the nonprofit sector has maintained a very significant role as well. In fact, the level of nonprofit expenditures on welfare services outdistances the levels of both federal government and state and local government expenditures on these same services. Far from withering away with the growth of government, the nonprofit sector seems to have blossomed as well.

ENDNOTES

"Far from withering away with the growth of government, the nonprofit sector seems to have blossomed as well."

1. For a statement of the theoretical rationale for this arrangement, see: Lester M. Salamon, "Of Market Failure, Government Failure, and Third-Party Government: Toward a Theory of Government-Nonprofit Relations in the Modern Welfare State," *Journal of Voluntary Action Research*, Vol. 16, Nos. 1 & 2 (January-June 1987), pp. 29-49.

2. "Social welfare services" are defined by the U.S. Social Security Administration as "the cash benefits, services, and administrative costs of public programs that directly benefit individuals and families." See: Ann Kallman Bixby, "Public Social Welfare Expenditures, Fiscal Years 1965-1987," *Social Security Bulletin*, Vol. 53, No. 2 (February 1990), p. 11. Unless otherwise noted, the data on government social welfare spending in this chapter are drawn from this source; from Ann Kallman Bixby, "Overview of Public Social Welfare Expenditures, Fiscal Year 1989," *Social Security Bulletin*, Vol. 54, No. 11 (November 1991); and from unpublished Social Security Administration data made available to the author.

3. The data reported here have been grouped somewhat differently from the way they are presented in the *Social Security Bulletin* data series cited in note 2, above. In particular, "pensions" here includes all of "social insurance" except Medicaid plus all of "veterans' programs" except for "veterans' health and medical programs" and veterans' education programs. "Income assistance" here includes "public aid" except for "vendor medical payments" (largely Medi-

caid) and "social services." Health includes "Health and medical programs" from the *Bulletin* listing plus Medicare and "vendor medical payments." "Education" here includes what is listed in the *Bulletin* under "education" plus what is listed under "veterans' education." "Social services" here includes what is listed in the *Bulletin* under "other social welfare" plus what is listed as "social services" under "public aid." These adjustments are needed to make the categories correspond more fully to the substantive program areas.

4. Based on data in Organization for Economic Cooperation and Development, *National Accounts, Detailed Tables, 1976-1988* (Paris: OECD, 1991).

5. Although it is difficult to draw firm conclusions about the consequences of these divergent spending patterns, at least some crucial social indicators suggest that at least some Americans pay a price for the country's generally lower rates of social welfare spending. For example, the United States ranks 23rd among the nations of the world in its rate of infant mortality, perhaps the best summary indicator of social well-being. England, Australia, Canada, Belgium, France, Denmark, Switzerland, the Netherlands, Japan, Sweden, and even the Soviet Union rank ahead of the United States on this important measure of social health. Similarly, the United States ranks 20th in life expectancy for men. *The New Book of World Rankings*.

How Did We Get Here? Historical Developments and Recent Trends

That the nonprofit sector retains a significant role in the American social welfare system is due in no small measure to how that system has evolved. At the same time, recent developments have exposed this sector to a variety of challenges and strains.

To understand the current position of the nonprofit sector in America's "mixed economy," therefore, it is necessary to understand how that "mixed economy" has evolved and what it has been experiencing in recent years.

To do so, this chapter is divided into two major sections. The first examines the two major eras of reform that gave rise to the mixed system of social welfare provision we have just described—one in the 1930s, which first established a significant governmental role, and the other in the 1960s, which expanded government's cooperation with the private, nonprofit sector. The second section then examines the strains to which the government–nonprofit partnership established in the 1960s and 1970s was exposed during the 1980s, and the challenges this poses for the future.

Historical Background[1]

The New Deal System

The basic foundation of America's current social welfare system was set during the New Deal era of the 1930s, much later than in most other industrialized countries. Prior to this, considerable popular sentiment in the United States opposed extensive government involvement, certainly extensive federal government involvement, in social welfare, and the task of responding to the poverty and distress created by the massive urbanization and industrialization of the late nineteenth and early twentieth centuries was left

"...the American social welfare system took shape through two principal eras of reform: one in the 1930s and the other in the mid-1960s. Yet neither established a truly comprehensive system of social welfare protection."

"...the United States emerged from the Second World War with a social welfare system that, despite the New Deal innovations, retained many features of the pre-New Deal era."

largely to local governments and private, charitable groups.

The Great Depression of the 1930s made clear, however, that such a private system of aid, however well intentioned, was not capable on its own to provide the protections that an urban–industrial society required. In response to the widespread distress of the depression era, President Franklin D. Roosevelt was therefore able to push through a system of public protections.

At the heart of the resulting New Deal system of social welfare aid were three principal programs:

- **Old age pensions** (the Social Security Program), financed largely by worker contributions to a Social Security Trust Fund;

- **Unemployment insurance**, providing temporary coverage for persons who lose their jobs, financed partly by worker contributions and partly by employer contributions; and

- **Cash assistance** (Old Age Assistance, Aid to Families with Dependent Children, Aid to the Blind) for specific categories of people considered unable to work and thus ineligible for help from the regular insurance programs (e.g., widows with young children).

These innovations represented major steps toward providing individuals some protection against the impersonal threats of an increasingly urban–industrial society. At the same time, however, because of the political opposition they faced, they were far from complete. Thus, neither Social Security nor Unemployment Insurance provided universal coverage. Eligibility was work-conditioned and even then extended only to certain types of workplaces (e.g., small businesses and farms were excluded). Cash assistance was available for those not covered by the social insurance programs, but it, too, was limited to narrow categories of people (widows with children, the aged, the blind), and responsibility for determining benefit levels and eligibility was vested in state governments, which were often quite restrictive.

As a consequence, the United States emerged from the Second World War with a social welfare system that, despite the New Deal innovations, retained many features of the pre-New Deal era. In particular, well into the 1960s the system remained characterized by:

- **Patchy coverage.** Key segments of the population remained uncovered, or inadequately protected. For example, expansion of Social Security coverage turned out to be much slower than hoped, so that farm workers, employees of small businesses, and others remained outside its protections. In addition, no assistance was available for health care costs. And welfare assistance, controlled by local officials, was held down so as not to interfere with wage rates on low-pay agricultural and household jobs, and was denied altogether to poor, intact families.

- **Limited funding.** Reflecting these limitations, spending on social welfare protections remained quite limited. As of 1950, for example, less than 9 percent of the U.S. gross national product was devoted to government social welfare spending.[2] Although some growth was evident in the 1950s, it was fairly limited, as shown in Figure 4.1.

- **State and local government dominance.** Despite the federal entrance in the 1930s, state and local governments continued to dominate the field. Well into the 1960s, state and local spending on social welfare outdistanced federal spending, as Figure 4.1 also shows.

- **Educational salience.** The major reason for the state and local prominence was that education continued to dominate the field, and education has traditionally been a state and local government function in the United States. As Figure 4.2 shows, up through the mid-1950s, education constituted the largest component of social welfare spending, accounting for 40 percent of the total. It was edged out slightly by pension benefits after that, but remained a very close second until the early 1970s.

FIGURE 4.1
Historical Trends in Government Social Welfare Spending, Total vs. Federal and State, 1950–1989: Current and Constant Dollars

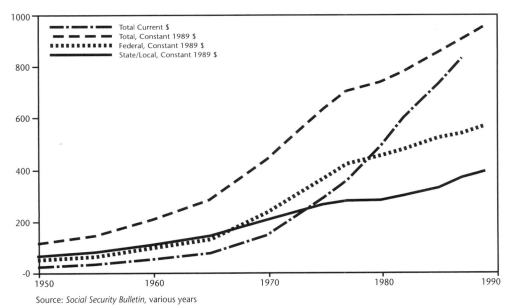

Legend:
- Total Current $
- Total, Constant 1989 $
- Federal, Constant 1989 $
- State/Local, Constant 1989 $

Source: *Social Security Bulletin,* various years

The "Great Society" System

These central features of the American social welfare system underwent a significant transformation in the 15 years between 1965 and 1980. Prompted by a wave of urban riots and evidence of continued, and deepening, poverty, a major effort was made during the "Great Society" era of the mid-1960s to complete the reforms of the 1930s and add to them in ways that would help the disadvantaged move into productive roles in society. This was followed in the early 1970s by a shift in the payment system in the basic Social Security program that turned out to have a profound impact on that program and on social welfare spending more generally. More particularly, the changes of this period included:

- creation in 1965 of a new national health insurance plan for the elderly (Medicare).
- creation in 1965 of a joint, federal-state program of health care for the poor (Medicaid).
- expansion of employment and training, social service, and housing aid for the disadvantaged.
- creation of a network of "Community Action Agencies" and preschool education programs in low-income neighborhoods.
- establishment in 1972 of an automatic cost-of-living adjustment in the basic Social Security program to adjust benefit levels automatically to inflation.

Coupled with shifts in the basic demographic contours of the population (in particular, an expan-

FIGURE 4.2
**Historical Trends in Government Social Welfare
Spending, by Field, 1950–1989, In Constant 1989 Dollars**

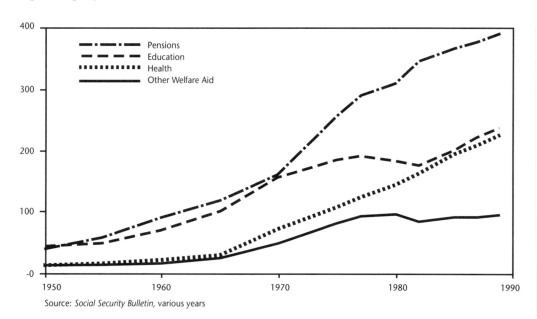

Source: *Social Security Bulletin,* various years

sion of the elderly population), these changes significantly reshaped the basic social welfare system, although in ways that are not fully understood. In particular, the system came to have the following distinguishing features:

- **Rapid growth in spending**. Between 1965 and 1980, government spending on social welfare accelerated significantly in the United States, as shown in Figure 4.1. Such spending grew by 637 percent in current dollars, and 263 percent in inflation-adjusted dollars. In the process, it expanded from 11.5 percent of gross national product in 1965 to 19.5 percent in 1976 before falling slightly to 18.5 percent as of 1980. During the first part of this period, 1965-1975, the principal source of growth was actual program expansion triggered by the creation of a host of new federal programs. Between 1975 and 1980, the principal source of growth was inflation, which boosted pension and health payments considerably.

- **Federal preeminence**. Around 1967, federal government spending on social welfare finally surpassed state and local government spending for the first time. What is more, it widened its lead subsequently, reaching over 60 percent of the total by 1980, as Figure 4.1 shows. Because the total was expanding as well, of course, this does not mean that the federal government *displaced* state and local governments, as we have already seen. But a significant shift in the relative positions did occur.

- **Relatively limited growth in aid to the poor.** Significantly, what accounted both for the overall growth in social welfare spending and the emergence of the federal government as the dominant player between 1965 and 1980 was *not* expanded welfare aid for the poor. Although such aid did grow, its rate of growth barely kept pace with the growth of other components of social welfare, as shown in Figure 4.2. By 1980, therefore, it still accounted for only 13 percent of all social welfare spending, compared to 12 percent 30 years earlier. This reflected the fact that (1) most Great Society "War on Poverty" programs were pilot efforts and few were fully funded; (2) the basic structure of welfare aid remained patchy and "categorical"— that is, available only to narrow categories of people, such as families headed by women with dependent children; and (3) only a few programs, such as Food Stamps, reached a broad cross section of the poor.

- **Predominance of pensions and health.** What mostly accounted for the great surge of spending that occurred in the 1965-1980 period, rather,

"Significantly, what accounted both for the overall growth in social welfare spending and the emergence of the federal government as the dominant player between 1965 and 1980 was not expanded welfare aid for the poor."

were the great middle-class programs, Social Security and health care (mostly Medicare). Total government spending on these two fields went from 48 percent of the total in 1950 to 62 percent in 1980, and this at a time when the overall total was growing massively. The reasons for this were several: (1) the size of the elderly population expanded considerably during this period; (2) medical costs, covered by the newly created Medicare program, accelerated thanks to technological changes and related factors; and (3) changes introduced in the Social Security program in 1972 provided automatic cost-of-living increases at a time when inflation was quite high.

Implications for Nonprofits: The Emergence of a Government-Nonprofit Partnership

The pattern of development of the American social welfare system detailed here had important implications for the evolution of the nation's private, nonprofit sector.

For one thing, the continued, patchy character of the public social welfare system established in the 1930s meant that private agencies continued to perform a significant role even after it had become clear during the Great Depression that primary reliance on private action was not sufficient.

Even more important, however, when public aid expanded in the 1960s, it often did so in ways that *promoted*, rather than displaced, the nonprofit sector. This was so because of the peculiar way government—particularly the federal government—operates in the United States. Because of ingrained American attitudes of hostility to centralized government, it is rare for the federal government to deliver services directly. Rather, it tends to operate through other entities—state governments, city governments, banks, other private businesses, and, increasingly in the 1960s, private nonprofit organizations. The result is an elaborate system of "third-party government," in which the national government generates the funds but then turns the actual delivery of services over to other public and private organizations.[3]

The private, nonprofit sector has been a major beneficiary of this mode of government operation. The upshot is an elaborate pattern of interrelationships between government and nonprofit organizations. For example:

- **Medicare**, the massive new federal health insurance program for the elderly created in 1965 essentially reimburses hospitals for care they provide to the elderly but leaves to the elderly the choice of which hospital to use. Because the preponderance

"...when public aid expanded in the 1960s, it often did so in ways that promoted, rather than displaced, the nonprofit sector. This was so because of America's peculiar system of 'third-party government,' in which the national government generates the funds but then turns the actual delivery of services over to other public and private organizations."

of hospital beds are in private, nonprofit hospitals, these institutions have received the preponderance of the benefits.

- Private, nonprofit universities have benefited from expanded federal **support for research**, as well as from new programs of scholarship aid and loan guarantees.

- New **social service and community development programs** provide grants-in-aid to state and local governments, which in turn often contract with local nonprofit organizations to provide such services as "meals on wheels" to the elderly, day care, residential care, adoption assistance, and the like.

As of 1980, therefore, approximately 25 percent of all government spending in the fields where nonprofit organizations were active flowed to such organizations. The federal government alone provided $40 billion in support to the private nonprofit sector that year, as shown in Table 4.1.[4] State and local governments were, in turn, providing additional amounts from their own resources. By comparison, total private charitable giving to these organizations that same year totalled $26.8 billion. No wonder the influential Commission on Private Philanthropy and Public Needs (the Filer Commission) concluded in the mid-1970s that government had become "a major 'philanthropist,' the major philanthropist in a number of the principal, traditional areas of philanthropy."[5] In fact, contrary to some beliefs, far from displacing the nonprofit sector, the expansion of government activity actually stimulated the growth of the nonprofit sector in the United States, equipping nonprofit organizations to carry out far more functions than they had been able to conduct in the past.

"...contrary to some beliefs, far from displacing the nonprofit sector, the expansion of government activity actually stimulated the growth of the nonprofit sector in the United States, equipping nonprofit organizations to carry out far more functions than they had been able to conduct in the past."

TABLE 4.1

Federal Government Support to Nonprofit Organizations, 1980 ($ billions)

Field	Amount	%
Health	$24.9	61%
Social Services	6.5	16
Education, research	5.6	14
Community development	2.3	6
Foreign aid	0.8	2
Arts, culture	0.3	1
Total	$40.4	100%

Source: Salamon and Abramson (1982), p. 43.

The 1980s: The Era of Retrenchment

Selective Retrenchment

After a decade and a half of rapid growth, government social welfare spending entered a period of retrenchment in the latter 1970s and into the 1980s. The initial impetus for this was a growth in federal deficits in the latter 1970s and an effort on the part of the Carter administration to restrain federal spending growth. Popular dissatisfaction with the apparent inefficacy of many of the Great Society social programs, fanned by conservative rhetoric, led in 1981, however, to a much more basic assault by the Reagan administration on at least a portion of the government social welfare program structure. Between 1977 and 1982, therefore, the inflation-adjusted value of federal spending dropped 5 percent in the income-assistance field, 29 percent in the social services field, and 33 percent in the education field, as shown in Table 4.2. Although it was hoped that state and local governments would offset these reductions, in fact the value of state and local government spending declined also in these fields. Outside of health and pensions, therefore, overall government social welfare spending declined by 8 percent in inflation-adjusted terms between 1977 and 1982.

Although Congress resisted further proposed cuts in the balance of the decade, a considerable slowing in the growth of government social welfare spending did occur, as reflected in Figure 4.3. While such spending expanded in real, inflation-adjusted terms by 149 percent in the twelve years between 1965 and 1977, or about 10 percent per year, it grew by a considerably slower 36 percent between 1977 and 1989, or less than 3 percent per year.

"...recent trends in government social welfare spending have posed serious problems for America's private, nonprofit organizations."

TABLE 4.2

Changes in Government Social Welfare Spending,
Fiscal Year 1982 vs. Fiscal Year 1977
(in constant dollars)*

Area	% Change, 1977-82		
	Federal	State/Local	Total
Pensions	16%	33%	19%
Health	31	26	29
Education	-33	-3	-8
Housing	19	47	22
Income assistance	-5	-16	-8
Social services	-29	-11	-23
Total	12%	6%	10%
Total w/o pensions & health	-15%	-5%	-8%

* Based on implicit price deflators for personal consumption expenditures.
Source: Compiled from data in *Social Security Bulletin*, Vol. 51, No. 4 (April 1988), pp. 23-26 and Vol. 46, No. 8 (August 1983), pp. 10-12. Implicit price deflators from *Economic Report of the President* (February 1991).

The slowdown was not universal, however. To the contrary, the retrenchment of the 1980s hit some programs more than others and missed some altogether, as Figure 4.3 also reveals. In particular:

- **Cuts concentrated in programs for the poor.** Programs targeted on the poor and low-income populations were the ones that experienced most of the cuts during this period. Thus, spending on income assistance programs dropped 4 percent in inflation-adjusted terms, and spending on other social services declined 19 percent.

- **Limited education gains.** Education spending also suffered from the cutbacks of the 1980s. Such spending barely kept pace with inflation during most of this period, growing by only about 1.5 percent per year until the very end of the decade. In fact, after adjusting for inflation, federal spending on education by 1989 was 28 percent below what it had been for 1977, and it was only growth at the state and local level that produced a net gain.

- **Continued growth in health spending.** While federal social service, income assistance, and education spending declined, however, federal health spending, fueled by escalating health costs and the aging of the population, continued its steep rise throughout this period of so-called retrenchment. Such spending grew by 81 percent between 1977 and 1989 even after adjusting for inflation.

- **Significant growth in pension expenditures.** Despite a steady decline in veterans' payments, pension expenditures also experienced continued growth during this period, rising by some 34 percent after adjusting for inflation. This was due to the automatic cost-of-living increases built into the Social Security program coupled with the continued growth of the elderly population.

- **Housing program expansion.** Alone among the programs at least moderately targeted on the poor, housing assistance experienced significant growth during this period. This reflects in part the low base from which it started and in part the commitments that had been entered into long before the Reagan administration came to power.

Put somewhat differently, of the $253 billion in real growth in government social welfare spending between 1977 and 1989, about 40 percent went for health, and another 38 percent went for old-age and veterans' pensions and unemployment insurance, as shown in Figure 4.4. These two components thus accounted for 78 percent of all the growth, even though they represented only 60 percent of the spending as of 1977. By contrast, income assistance and other social service programs experienced not only no growth, but actual declines. The overall effect

FIGURE 4.3
Changes in Government Social Welfare Spending, 1977–1989 vs. 1965–1977, in Constant 1987 Dollars

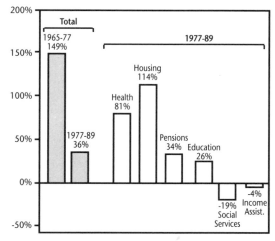

Source: See Table 4.2 and Figure 4.1.

"The overall effect [of the Reagan reforms] was to shift the center of gravity of the social welfare system more toward the middle class and away from the poor."

was thus to shift the center of gravity of the social welfare system more toward the middle class and away from the poor.

Implications for the Nonprofit Sector

In justifying these changes, the Reagan administration suggested that cutbacks in government social welfare spending would create more opportunities for private, nonprofit organizations. To those who pointed out that such organizations relied extensively on government support to enable them to carry out their existing functions, the administration expressed the hope that private giving would fill any resulting gap.

To what extent have these hopes and expectations come to fruition? How has the nonprofit sector fared during the decade of the 1980s? The answer is somewhat mixed.[6]

Overall growth. In the first place, as shown in Figure 4.5, the nonprofit sector did experience continued growth during the 1977-1989 period. In fact, the sector outpaced the growth of government social welfare spending during this period, growing by 79 percent after adjusting for inflation compared to the 36 percent growth in overall government social welfare spending.

Uneven growth. In the second place, however, this growth was very uneven. As Figure 4.5 also makes clear, nonprofit health organizations grew by 92 percent during this period, whereas social service and civic and social organizations added only 62 percent and 35 percent, respectively, to their revenues, and most of this came at the end of the period, following many years of decline. In fact, as Figure 4.6 shows,

> *"The decade of the 1980s witnessed a further shift of the center of gravity of the nonprofit sector away from social services and toward health."*

FIGURE 4.4
Shares of Government Social Welfare Spending Growth, by Major Field, 1977–1989

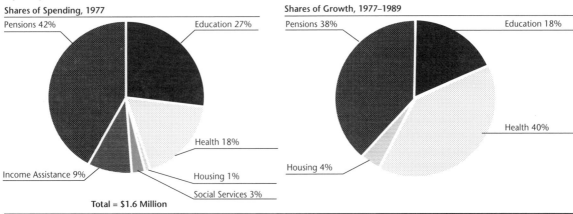

Shares of Spending, 1977

Pensions 42%
Education 27%
Health 18%
Housing 1%
Social Services 3%
Income Assistance 9%
Total = $1.6 Million

Shares of Growth, 1977–1989

Pensions 38%
Education 18%
Health 40%
Housing 4%

Source: See Figure 4.1 and Table 4.2.

health organizations, which accounted for 52 percent of all nonprofit expenditures when this period began, accounted for 60 percent of the growth. By contrast, social and legal service organizations, which accounted for 12 percent of all revenues at the start of the period, claimed only 9 percent of the growth. The decade of the 1980s thus witnessed a further shift of the center of gravity of the nonprofit sector away from social services and toward health.

Shifts in sources of support. This pattern, finally, reflected the significant shifts that occurred in the revenue base of the nonprofit sector. In the first place, the hoped-for surge in private, charitable support did not occur. Although private giving did grow—by about 53 percent in inflation-adjusted terms—its growth actually lagged behind that of most of the other sources of nonprofit income. Private giving, which accounted for 18 percent of nonprofit income as of 1977, accounted for only 15 percent of the overall growth of the nonprofit sector between 1977 and 1989, as shown in Figure 4.7.

Instead of private giving, the major source of nonprofit growth during this period was service fees and other commercial income. This source alone accounted for over half of all the growth of the sector between 1977 and 1989, compared to the 47 percent of all income that it represented as of 1977.

Finally, nonprofit receipts from government continued to grow. This income grew by 46 percent after adjusting for inflation between 1977 and 1989 and accounted for 30 percent of the sector's growth. In other words, the government share of nonprofit income held fairly steady throughout this period. However, the composition of the government support changed significantly. In particular, most of this growth was concentrated in the health field. In fact, over 80 percent of all the government support that the nonprofit sector gained between 1977 and 1989 went to nonprofit health providers.

Summary

The American social welfare system is a complex "mixed economy" of federal, state, and local government, private for-profit, and private nonprofit activity. Although sizable governmental expenditures are made for social welfare, much of this goes for old-age pensions, veterans' payments, and public schools. Expenditures for the poor and the disadvantaged, by contrast, represent only a fraction of the total, albeit still a sizable amount.

Alongside the governmental system, moreover, stands a private nonprofit one that rivals at least the public welfare portion of the governmental system in

FIGURE 4.5
Changes in Nonprofit Revenues, by Subsector, 1977–1989, in Constant 1989 Dollars*

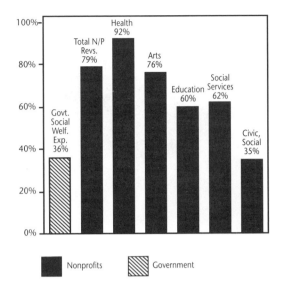

Source: Compiled from data in Hodgkinson, Weitzman, et. al. (1992), p. 147.
*Based on Personal Consumption Expenditure Implicit Price deflator.

FIGURE 4.6
Shares of Nonprofit Growth, 1977–1989, by Type of Agency

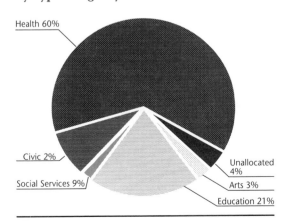

Source: See Figure 4.5.

FIGURE 4.7
Sources of Nonprofit Growth, 1977–1989

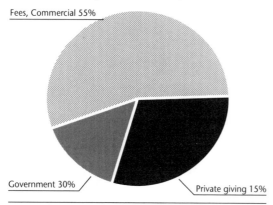

Fees, Commercial 55%

Government 30%

Private giving 15%

Source: See Figure 4.5.

size. Private philanthropy plays an important part in supporting this nonprofit system, but government and fees play an even larger part.

Recent changes in government spending have placed considerable strains on both of these systems. The nonprofit sector has been significantly affected by these changes, although the impact has been disguised somewhat by the aggregate totals. Thus, while the sector as a whole has grown, most of the growth has been concentrated in a few areas—principally health and education. These sectors have grown, first, because they have access to fee income, and second, because the government support flowing to them has been much less affected by the budget stringency of the past few years. By contrast, social service agencies have been under more severe budgetary strain.

What these observations make clear, among other things, is that the American social welfare system cannot be understood at the aggregate level alone. To make sense of what is going on, it is necessary to move from the overview provided in this section to a more in-depth look at some of the major subsectors, and at the public and private roles in each. We turn to this task in the chapters that follow, beginning with the largest subfield, health.

ENDNOTES

1. The discussion in this section draws on material in Lester M. Salamon, *Welfare: The Elusive Consensus —Where We Are, How We Got Here, and What's Ahead* (New York: Praeger Publishers, 1977).

2. Bixby (1990), p. 22.

3. For further elaboration of this point, see: Lester M. Salamon, "Rethinking Public Management: Third-Party Government and the Changing Forms of Government Action," *Public Policy* (1981), Vol. 29, pp. 255-275; and Lester M. Salamon, *Beyond Privatization: The Tools of Government Action* (Washington: The Urban Institute Press, 1989); Ralph Kramer, *Voluntary Agencies in the Welfare State* (Berkeley, CA: University of California Press, 1981). For a discussion of a similar phenomenon in the United Kingdom, see: Jennifer Wolch, *The Shadow State* (New York: The Foundation Center, 1990).

4. Lester M. Salamon and Alan J. Abramson, *The Nonprofit Sector and the New Federal Budget* (Washington: The Urban Institute Press, 1986), p. 62.

5. Commission on Philanthropy and Public Needs. *Giving in America: Toward a Stronger Voluntary Sector* (Washington: Commission on Private Philanthropy and Public Needs, 1975), p. 89.

6. For more detail on the Reagan program and its implications for the nonprofit sector, see: Lester M. Salamon and Alan J. Abramson, "The Nonprofit Sector," in *The Reagan*

Revolution, John L. Palmer and Isabel Sawhill, eds., (Washington: The Urban Institute Press, 1982), pp. 219-243; and Lester M. Salamon, "Nonprofit Organizations: The Lost Opportunity," in *The Reagan Record*, John L. Palmer and Isabel Sawhill, eds., (Cambridge, MA: Ballinger Publishing Co., 1984), pp. 261-286.

PART TWO

Key Subsectors — Public and Private Roles

CHAPTER FIVE

Health Care

Of all the components of the nonprofit service sector, the largest by far is health care. As Chapter Two indicated, nonprofit health providers absorbed close to 60 percent of *all* nonprofit revenues, and just over 25 percent of all private *charitable* revenues, in 1989. This reflects the tremendous scale of the health care field. But it also reflects the substantial role that nonprofit organizations play in this field.

The purpose of this chapter is to explore this nonprofit role in the health field and to put it into context in relation to the position of government and for-profit health providers.

To do so, we begin by looking more closely at the overall scale and character of health care expenditures in the United States. We then zero in on the three subfields where nonprofit providers are particularly prominent: (1) hospital care, (2) nursing home care, and (3) in-home or outpatient clinic care. In each of these subfields, we seek to determine what role non-profit providers play, how this compares with the role of government and for-profit providers, and what the major trends have been in recent years.

Perhaps the central conclusion that emerges from this analysis is that the nation's health care system depends critically on the nonprofit sector.

"What emerges most clearly from this analysis is the conclusion that the nation's health care system depends critically on the nonprofit sector."

Overview: National Health Spending

Basic Contours

Current scale. Health has emerged in recent years as one of the largest and fastest growing components of national spending. As Chapter Three made clear, almost one in four dollars of government social welfare spending goes for health care, and an even larger amount of private spending goes into this field as well. As of 1988, in fact, health care accounted for

Although government spending on health grew faster than private spending between 1965 and 1988, close to 60 percent of health spending still comes from private sources. Very little of this private revenue comes from private philanthropy, however.

11.1 percent of the U.S. gross national product—a total of $540 billion in spending.

Sources. Of this total, government health expenditures account for only 42 percent—well above what it was 20 years earlier, but still well below half. The balance of health spending—58 percent of the total—came from private sources, most of it fees and private insurance payments (see Table 5.1).[1]

Growth. Health expenditures are not only large, but they have also been growing rapidly. As Table 5.1 shows, total health spending grew thirteenfold between 1965 and 1988, compared to a sevenfold increase in the nation's gross national product. As a result, health expenditures went from about 6 percent of gross national product in 1965 to 11 percent by 1988.

Sources of growth. A principal source of this growth, as Table 5.1 shows, was the increase that occurred in government health spending. Government health spending grew 22-fold between 1965 and 1988, compared to a tenfold increase in private health spending. This reflects primarily the creation of the federal Medicare and Medicaid programs in 1965. As a result, government spending on health increased from 25 percent of the total in 1965 to 42 percent of a much larger total in 1988. In terms of absolute dollars, however, the private-sector contribution to the growth was even larger, so that private sources remained the dominant funder, accounting for close to 60 percent of the total expenditures as of 1988.

The Nonprofit Sector and Health

Role of philanthropy. Very little of this private revenue comes from private philanthropy, however. Of the $540 billion in health care spending in 1988, only

TABLE 5.1
U.S. Health Care Spending, 1965-1988 ($ billions)

Source	1965 Amount	1965 %	1988 Amount	1988 %	% Change 1965-1988
Private	$31.3	75%	$312.4	58%	+998%
Government	10.3	25	227.5	42	2209
Total	$41.6	100%	$539.9	100%	+1300%
GNP	705.0		4,881		692%
Health as % of GNP		5.9%		11.1%	

Source: *Health Care Financing Review*, Vol. II, No. 4 (Summer 1990), p. 24.

$24 billion, or less than 5 percent, came from private philanthropic giving. Clearly, private philanthropy plays a relatively limited role overall in the financing of health care. Such giving is considerably more important in selected aspects of the health field, however. As we will see more fully later, private philanthropy accounts for 9 percent of the income of health clinics and 6 percent of health construction and research.

Role of the nonprofit sector. While private philanthropy may play a relatively limited role in the *financing* of health services, the private, nonprofit sector plays a very significant role in the *delivery* of health services. To understand this role, however, it is necessary to divide the health sector into its component parts and look more closely at the three components where nonprofit organizations are most important: hospital care, nursing home care, and clinic care.

Hospital Care

Overview
Hospital care represents the largest single component of health care in the United States, and also the one where nonprofit organizations are most prominent.

Scale. As Figure 5.1 shows, close to 40 percent of all health spending goes for hospital care—a total of $212 billion in 1988. By comparison, private practitioners (dentists and physicians) received 25 percent of the total and nursing homes, 8 percent.

Sources of funding. Unlike other components of the health care field, government is the dominant source of funding for hospitals. Slightly over half of all hospital revenue comes from government, with the federal government contributing 41 percent of the total in

FIGURE 5.1
Where Health Spending Goes, 1988

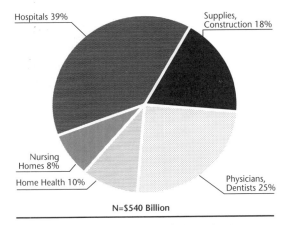

N=$540 Billion

Source: *Health Care Financing Review*, Vol. 11, No. 4 (Summer 1990), Table 15, p. 30.

"While private philanthropy may play a relatively limited role in the financing of health services, the private, nonprofit sector plays a very significant role in the delivery of health services."

FIGURE 5.2
Sources of Health Care Spending, 1988

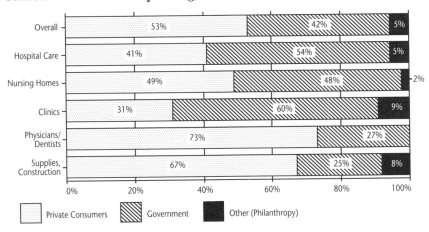

FIGURE 5.3
Types of Hospitals, 1989

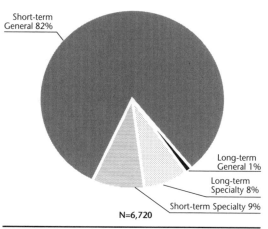

Short-term
General 82%

Long-term
General 1%

Long-term
Specialty 8%

Short-term Specialty 9%

N=6,720

Source: American Hospital Association, *Hospital Statistics 1990/91.*
Tables 2A and 2B, pp. 8–13.

FIGURE 5.4
Nonprofit Share of Hospital Industry, 1989

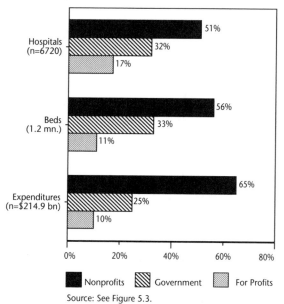

Hospitals
(n=6720)
51%
32%
17%

Beds
(1.2 mn.)
56%
33%
11%

Expenditures
(n=$214.9 bn)
65%
25%
10%

0%   20%   40%   60%   80%

■ Nonprofits   ▨ Government   ▨ For Profits

Source: See Figure 5.3.

1988 and state and local governments contributing 13 percent. The remaining funding, about 46 percent in 1988, comes from private sources, including 5 percent from private philanthropy and 41 percent from private fees (see Figure 5.2).

Types of hospitals. As of 1989, there were about 6,720 hospitals registered with the American Hospital Association in the United States. Of these, the overwhelming majority (82 percent) were short-term, general hospitals, the type with which most people are familiar (see Figure 5.3). The remainder included about 550 short-term specialized hospitals (e.g., psychiatric hospitals) and 535 long-term hospitals, most of them also specialty institutions.[2]

Nonprofit, Government, and For-Profit Roles in the Hospital Industry

Nonprofit hospitals. All three sectors—government, private business, and the nonprofit sector—play a role in the hospital field. But the nonprofit role is clearly dominant. As reflected in Figure 5.4, just over half (51 percent) of all hospitals in the country are organized as nonprofits. These nonprofit hospitals account for 56 percent of the country's hospital beds, and nearly two-thirds (65 percent) of all hospital expenditures. Nonprofits are especially prominent among short-term, general hospitals, which, as we have seen, are the center of gravity of the hospital industry. Fifty-five percent of these institutions are private, nonprofit organizations; and they tend to be the larger institutions, so that nonprofits account for 65 percent of short-term, general hospital *beds* and 69 percent of the short-term, general hospital *expenditures*. By contrast, nonprofits generally play a smaller role among specialty hospitals, for example, psychiatric, tuberculosis, chronic disease, and rehabilitation hospitals. Among these latter, nonprofits account for only 28 percent of the institutions and 14 percent of the beds.

Government hospitals. About a third of all hospitals are operated by governmental authorities, chiefly at the state and local levels (see Figure 5.4). Most of these are short-term, general hospitals, many of them in central city areas. However, relative to the other two sectors, the government role is particularly prominent in the operation of long-term, specialized hospitals, such as those for the mentally ill. Nearly 60 percent of long-term psychiatric hospitals, for example, are under government ownership and control, and they account for 77 percent of all the long-term care facility expenditures. More generally, government accounts for 32 percent of all specialty hospitals, but because these facilities tend to be large, they represent 54 percent of all specialty hospital expenditures and 70 percent of specialty hospital beds.

For-profit hospitals. For-profit corporations play a considerably smaller role in the hospital field, with 17 percent of all hospitals and 11 percent of all hospital beds (see Figure 5.4). However, for-profit corporations have carved out a niche among specialty hospitals, particularly short-term psychiatric hospitals, 70 percent of which are for-profit institutions. More generally, for profits account for 40 percent of all specialty hospitals and 16 percent of all specialty hospital beds.

Hospital Trends

Overall decline. Despite the substantial growth in hospital expenditures, the hospital sector has been under considerable strain in recent years as efforts have been made to constrain the growth of both public and private health costs. Reflecting this, between 1980 and 1989, both the total number of hospitals and the total number of hospital beds declined in the United States, the former by 4 percent and the latter by 11 percent (see Figure 5.5).

Variation among types. As Figure 5.5 makes clear, however, not all segments of the hospital industry were affected equally by these pressures. As a general rule, government hospitals have suffered the sharpest declines, for-profit hospitals have experienced considerable growth, and nonprofit hospitals have just about held their own. Let us look more closely at these divergent patterns and the changes that lie behind them.

Sharp decline of government hospitals. The contraction in the hospital industry between 1980 and 1989 was especially marked among government institutions. Between 1980 and 1989, the number of government-owned and -operated hospitals declined by 17 percent, and the number of beds in government-owned hospitals declined by 28 percent.

Two major developments lie behind these results:

- First, increased pressure on publicly run, inner-city hospitals squeezed by rising health costs, reduced Medicaid reimbursement, and limited fee income. As a result, 359 of the 2,167 publicly owned, short-term, general hospitals were forced to close between 1980 and 1989.

- Second, a movement that began in the 1970s away from the institutionalization of mentally ill and other long-term ill persons in massive, publicly run facilities. The number of government-run specialty hospitals declined by nearly 40 percent between 1970 and 1989 as a result of this "deinstitutionalization" policy, and the number of beds in such facilities declined by over 70 percent.

FIGURE 5.5
Hospital Trends, by Ownership, 1980–1989

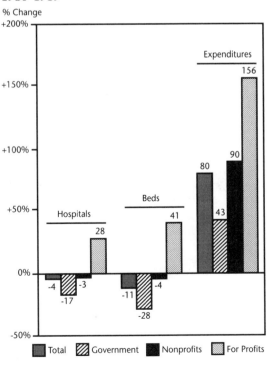

Source: See Figure 5.3.

Contraction among short-term general hospitals.
The sharp decline of inner-city government hospitals
was itself part of a broader contraction that affected
short-term hospitals more generally during the 1980s.
Overall, the number of short-term general hospitals
declined by 8 percent during this decade, and the
number of short-term general hospital beds declined
by 6 percent. Although this hit public hospitals particularly hard, nonprofit general hospitals were also
affected, producing a net decline of 4 percent in the
number of such hospitals, and of 5 percent in the
number of beds they provided.

Overall growth of short-term specialty hospitals.
Notwithstanding the overall decline in the number of
hospitals and the particular drop in the number of
long-term government specialty hospitals, specialty
hospitals as a group experienced significant growth
during the 1980s. This was especially true among
short-term specialty hospitals—for the mentally ill,
rehabilitation patients, and patients with other specialized diseases. The number of such hospitals grew
by almost 80 percent between 1980 and 1989, and the
number of beds they were able to offer almost dou-
bled. What seems to have been under way, in short, is
a movement away from large-scale general hospitals
toward specialized hospitals, and from long-term
institutionalized treatment to shorter-term hospitalization coupled with in-home care.

Expansion of for-profit providers. For-profit businesses have been particularly prominent in these
shifts. Of the 239 short-term specialty hospitals added
in the 1980s, over three-fourths were for-profit companies, and these companies accounted for 70 percent
of the net gain in short-term specialty hospital beds.
For-profit businesses also gained ground in the other
components of the hospital industry as well, moreover, adding short-term general and long-term facilities and beds also. Overall, therefore, the number of
for-profit hospitals increased by almost 30 percent
during this decade, and the number of beds they controlled increased by more than 40 percent. In the process, the for-profit component of the hospital industry went from 13 percent of the facilities in 1980 to 17
percent in 1989.

Implications for nonprofits. These trends have naturally had important implications for nonprofit hospitals. Most significantly, as we have seen, the pressures
on short-term general hospitals have caused a contraction in the number of short-term nonprofit institutions and beds. In addition, the number of nonprofit long-term facilities and beds has also declined.
However, nonprofits have also taken part in the gen-

*"Hospital care represents the largest single
component of health care in the United
States, and also the one where nonprofit
organizations are most prominent."*

*"What seems to have been under way
[during the past decade] is a movement
away from large-scale general hospitals...
and from long-term institutionalized
treatment to shorter-term hospitalization
coupled with in-home care. For-profit
businesses have been particularly
prominent in these shifts."*

eral expansion of short-term specialty hospitals. The number of such nonprofit institutions increased by 38 percent between 1980 and 1989, and the number of beds they accounted for increased by 41 percent. What this suggests is that nonprofits are experiencing pressures and being forced to consolidate in their traditional area of concentration—short-term, general hospitals—but are also venturing out into the more rapidly growing field of short-term specialty care where for-profit hospitals have been particularly active and effective.

Clinics and Home Health Care

Overview

The second largest component of the health field in which nonprofit organizations have a substantial role is home health and specialized clinic care. This component of the health care field accounted for 10 percent of all health expenditures in 1988, or about $52 billion, as shown in Figure 5.1.

Of this total, about one-third goes for *government public health activities,* which includes local public health screening and the federal government's Public Health Service and Center for Disease Control. An even larger share (43 percent) went for a variety of *outpatient clinics* (e.g., kidney dialysis centers, drug treatment centers, rehabilitation centers). This component bears strong resemblance to the short-term specialty institutions that are gaining ground within the hospital industry, except that these facilities are tailored to "outpatient" care. Another 8 percent of this portion of health care spending went for the relatively new field of *home health care* (i.e., skilled nursing or medical care provided in the home), a field that has some resemblance to traditional social services. Finally, the remaining 20 percent went for *other personal health services*, such as drug abuse treatment and school health.

Nonprofit Role

Nonprofit organizations play a major role in the provision of outpatient and home health care, although they have recently faced considerable competition from for-profit providers, just as they have in the related field of short-term specialty hospital care. In addition to the government-operated health clinics, the U.S. Census Bureau identified 28,383 private health clinics and related service facilities in its latest Census of Service Industries in 1987. Of this total, 21,316 were home health providers and specialized clinics (e.g., blood banks, kidney dialysis centers), and 7,067 were clinics (as opposed to individual offices) of

"Nonprofit organizations play a major role in the provision of outpatient and home health care, although they have recently faced considerable competition from for-profit providers, just as they have in the related field of short-term specialty hospital care."

FIGURE 5.6
Nonprofit Share of Private Clinics and Other Health Services, 1987

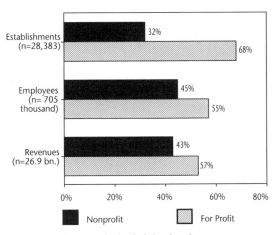

Source: Author's calculations based upon
U.S. Census of Service Industries, 1987, Tables 1A and 1B.

doctors and dentists.[3]

Of these 28,383 clinics, about one-third (32 percent) are private, *nonprofit* institutions, and two-thirds are *for-profit* companies, as shown in Figure 5.6. The nonprofit firms tend to be slightly larger, however, so they accounted for 45 percent of the employees and 43 percent of the revenues.

Recent Trends

The outpatient care field has been an extremely dynamic one in recent years, and nonprofit providers have hardly been immune from the resulting shifts. Two major forces of change in particular have been evident: first, a particularly rapid growth in expenditures; and second, increased competition from for-profit providers.

Growth in spending. Despite the rapid pace of growth in overall health spending between 1975 and 1988, the pace of growth in outpatient care and home health spending still exceeded it by a substantial margin, as shown in Figure 5.7. Thus, compared to an increase of 94 percent in the inflation-adjusted value of overall health expenditures between 1975 and 1988, spending on outpatient care grew by 208 percent, and spending on home health care grew by 450 percent.

FIGURE 5.7
Recent Trends in Clinic and Home Health Care, 1975–1988

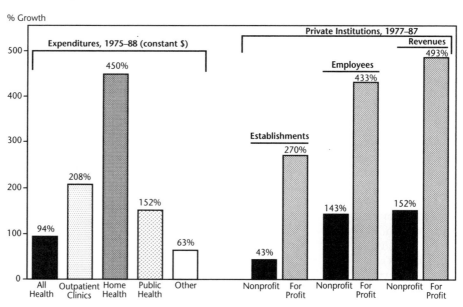

Source: *Health Care Financing Review*, 1990; 1977 and 1987
U.S. Census of Service Industries.

Both of these developments reflected the move toward deinstitutionalization of long-term hospital patients during the 1970s and early 1980s, which increased the need for home health care and specialty, outpatient clinic care. Also at work were the pressures being put on hospitals by a shift in the Medicare reimbursement system, which induced hospitals to release patients earlier and produced a corresponding increased need for outpatient care facilities. Finally, these changes were aided by the broadening of government medical reimbursement for home health care services, 75 percent of which were funded by government by 1988.[4]

Increased competition from for-profit providers. Interestingly, nonprofit providers have benefited far less from these changes than have for-profit ones. The past decade has witnessed an explosion of for-profit involvement in the outpatient clinic and home health field. Although nonprofits have not lost ground in absolute terms, they certainly have relatively, losing their once-dominant position in this field. As Figure 5.7 shows, for example, between 1977 and 1987 the number of *for-profit* outpatient clinics and related health service establishments increased by 270 percent, the number of people they employed increased 433 percent, and the revenues they received increased by 493 percent. By contrast, the respective increases for *nonprofit providers* in these fields were 43 percent, 143 percent, and 152 percent. In the process, nonprofits dropped from 55 percent of the establishments and 64 percent of the employees in 1977 to 32 percent of the establishments and 45 percent of the employees ten years later. Clearly, as institutionalized medical care has moved out of large, general-purpose hospitals and long-term specialized care facilities into specialized clinics and other short-term specialized care facilities, many more for-profit firms have been attracted into the field. Although nonprofit organizations retain a considerable, and still-growing, role, they are encountering increasingly stiff competition.

Nursing Home Care

Overview
Nursing home care is the third major component of the health field where nonprofit organizations are active. As noted in Figure 5.1, nursing homes absorbed about 8 percent of all health spending in 1988, a total of some $43 billion. Of this, about half comes from private sources, all but 1 percent in the form of fees; the other half comes from government, largely through the Medicaid program for the poor (see Figure 5.2).

"The past decade has witnessed an explosion of for-profit involvement in the outpatient clinic and home-health field."

FIGURE 5.8
Nonprofit Share of Nursing Home Industry, 1986/87

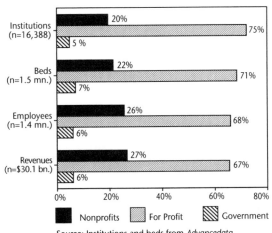

Source: Institutions and beds from *Advancedata*, No. 147 (January 22, 1988); employees and revenue from *U.S. Census of Service Industries*, 1987.

Nonprofit versus Government and For-Profit Roles

Unlike the hospital and outpatient clinic portions of the health field, nonprofit organizations play a subsidiary role in the nursing home industry. Of the 16,388 nursing homes identified in the 1986 Inventory of Long-Term Care Places (ILTCP), *nonprofits* accounted for only 20 percent, as shown in Figure 5.8.[5] By contrast, 75 percent of the nursing homes are *for-profit institutions*, and 5 percent are under *government* control. Because the nonprofit institutions tend to be somewhat larger, they represent a slightly larger proportion of the beds, employees, and revenues (22 percent, 26 percent, and 27 percent, respectively), but for-profit providers dominate in these spheres as well. Even so, nonprofits are still a considerable force in the nursing home industry, with some 4,000 homes, 330,000 beds, and $8.2 billion in revenues.

Trends

Unlike the situation in the outpatient care field, for-profit dominance in the nursing home industry is not a recent development. As of the late 1960s, for example, 72 percent of the nursing and related care homes identified by the National Master Facility Inventory were already under for-profit control.[6] The two decades since then, however still produced some important changes.

FIGURE 5.9
Nursing Home Trends, 1969–1980 vs. 1977–1987

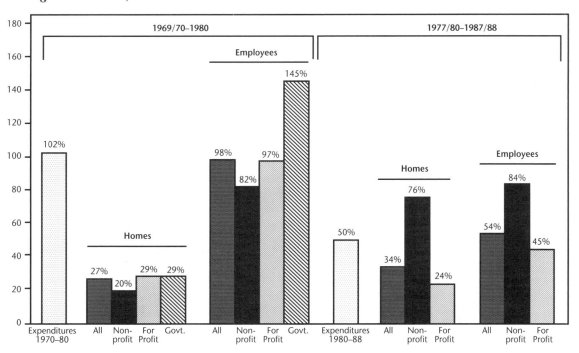

Source: *Health Care Financing Review*, Summer 1991; Strahan, 1984; 1977 and 1987 *Census of Service Industries.*

The growth decade of the 1970s. The period follow-ing the creation of the Medicaid program in 1965 was one of considerable growth in the nursing home industry. As Figure 5.9 shows, nursing home expendi-tures grew by more than 100 percent in inflation-adjusted terms during this decade, the total number of homes increased by 27 percent, and the total num-ber of employees grew by 98 percent. At the same time, the number of nursing home beds increased by 75 percent. These trends reflected the aging of the population and the availability of government fund-ing to cope with the resulting need.

Interestingly, while all segments of the nursing home industry participated in this growth, for-profit homes expanded most rapidly. Between 1969 and 1980, the number of homes under the control of pro-prietary institutions rose by 29 percent, compared to only 20 percent for nonprofits. Similarly, the number of employees and beds at the proprietary homes increased by 97 percent and 84 percent, respectively, compared to only 82 percent and 52 percent for non-profit homes. As a consequence, for-profits strength-ened their already dominant position in the industry, even though nonprofit homes expanded as well.

"Most hospitals, about a third of the clinics, as well as one in four nursing homes, are private, nonprofit organizations."

The constrained decade of the 1980s. A different dynamic seems to have been at work during the decade of the 1980s. In the first place, the growth of government support slowed considerably, as both the federal government and state and local governments sought to reduce the escalating costs of Medicaid, even though the need for nursing home services con-tinued to grow. Thus, as shown in Figure 5.9, nursing home expenditures grew by only 50 percent between 1980 and 1988 compared to its 102 percent real growth between 1970 and 1980.

Faced with this constraint in public support, the for-profit and nonprofit components of the nursing home industry seem to have responded somewhat dif-ferently. Whereas for-profit homes expanded more extensively during the 1970s, it was the nonprofit firms that moved to meet the demand in the con-strained climate of the 1980s. Thus, as Figure 5.9 shows, the number of nonprofit homes increased by 76 percent between 1977 and 1987 compared to 24 percent for for-profit providers. Similarly, the number of employees at nonprofit homes grew by 84 percent during this more recent period, compared to a 45 per-cent growth among for-profit homes. As a result, the nonprofit sector boosted its share of the nursing home industry during this period, from 22 percent of all employees in 1977 to 26 percent in 1987.[7]

The explanation for this pattern is not entirely clear. But one plausible explanation is that the non-

"Whereas for-profit [nursing] homes expanded more extensively during the 1970s, it was the nonprofit firms that moved to meet the demand in the constrained climate of the 1980s."

profit sector functioned during this era the way the theories surrounding its role would suggest: It responded to needs even after economic prospects dimmed, very likely drawing on the resources of religious and other charitable institutions.

Other Health Activities

Nonprofit organizations play a far less significant role in the remaining aspects of the health care field identified in Figure 5.1: physician services and supplies, and miscellaneous. Both of these are quite substantial areas, accounting, respectively, for 25 percent and 18 percent of all health spending.

Physician services. So far as physician services are concerned, except for the clinics and outpatient facilities identified earlier, these are typically handled in the offices of private practitioners, and these offices are treated as for-profit businesses. As of 1987, there were 357,812 such offices, as compared with 28,383 clinics and 425,859 health establishments of all kinds (see Table 5.2). Private doctors' offices thus represented 94 percent of the physician service facilities and 84 percent of *all* health facilities. In terms of employees and revenues, private doctors' offices represent a smaller share of the total (21 percent of all private health employees and 27 percent of all private health receipts), but they remain a significant component of the American health scene.

Supplies, construction, and research. Much of the provision of hospital supplies is also handled by for-profit firms. However, nonprofits do play a role in medical research, much of it through government-sponsored research at private colleges and universities, which will be dealt with in the next chapter. In addition, *philanthropic giving* has traditionally played a major role in hospital and other health facility construction, even though it has not in the provision of basic health care. Overall, more than 6 percent of health research and construction was financed by

TABLE 5.2

Private Doctors Offices vs. Clinics and All Private Health Providers, 1987

	Establishments	Employees (millions)	Revenues ($bn)
Private doctors offices	357,812	1.742	$120.3
Clinics	23,383	0.705	26.9
Total	381,195	2.447	147.2
Private offices as %	94%	71%	82%
All private health providers	425,859	8.240	449.8
Doctors offices as %	84%	21%	27%

Source: *1987 Census of Service Industries,* Tables 1a and 1b.

philanthropy in 1988, although this was significantly less than the 26 percent covered from this source in 1960, before the establishment of government programs to help finance these functions.[8]

Conclusion

The health care sector is thus the largest component of the American social welfare system outside of old age pensions. It is, moreover, a complex sector, containing many different types of institutions and multiple sources of funds. The primary access to this complex system for most people is through private practitioners operating as for-profit businesses. But much of the institutional care is provided through nonprofit organizations. Although for-profit firms have recently made significant inroads here as well, nonprofits still account for over half of the hospital care, 40 percent of the outpatient clinic care, and a quarter of the nursing home care. They thus form a vital part of the nation's health care delivery system and have demonstrated durability in the face of rather dramatic recent changes.

"Of all the components of the nonprofit service sector, the largest by far is the health care component."

The public sector also plays a major role in the health care system but less as a deliverer of services than as a *financer* of them. About 40 percent of overall health expenditures, over half of all hospital care, close to 60 percent of all clinic care, and about half of nursing home care is financed with public funds.

In short, the health field provides an excellent example of the "mixed economy" and public-private partnership that lies at the heart of the American social welfare system, with nonprofit, for-profit, and governmental institutions all playing vital roles, often in close collaboration with each other.

ENDNOTES

1. "National Health Expenditures, 1988," *Health Care Financing Review* (Summer 1990), Vol. 11, No. 4, Table 13, p. 24.

2. American Hospital Association, *Hospital Statistics 1990/91*, Tables 2A and 2B.

3. The category "clinics of doctors and dentists" was included in the 1987 Census tabulations for the first time. Such clinics are defined as "general medical clinics staffed by licensed practitioners having M.D. degree" and "not owned and operated by physicians associated for the purpose of carrying on their profession." We assume that at least some of these clinics were included in earlier censuses of service industries as "outpatient care facilities" or "other health and allied services, not elsewhere classified." For our purposes here, therefore, we added them in with other types of clinics. The breakdown between for-profit and nonprofit entities is approximately the same in 1987 for these clinics of doctors and dentists as it is for the

more narrow category of "other health service" organizations. See: U.S. Bureau of the Census, *1987 Census of Service Industries,* Appendix A, p. A-16. (Washington: U.S. Government Printing Office, 1989).

4. Based on data in *Health Care Financing Review* (Summer 1990), p. 30.

5. The definition of what constitutes a nursing home is somewhat complicated. Generally speaking, nursing homes are facilities providing skilled nursing care or residential facilities in which medical care is a significant component of the care. Other residential facilities, such as half-way houses, are generally treated differently, although such facilities were covered by the 1986 Inventory of Long-Term Care Places (ILTCP). The ILTCP total count of nursing homes, as opposed to "residential facilities," was 16,388 as of 1986. By comparison, the U.S. Census Bureau counted 17,525 private establishments alone in its 1987 Census of Service Industries. In all likelihood, the census survey included some mental retardation facilities that were excluded from the ILTCP count. For information on the ILTCP survey, see: Al Sirrocco, "Nursing and Related Care Homes as Reported from the 1986 Inventory of Long-Term Care Places," *Advancedata,* No. 147 (January 22, 1988). For information on the Census of Service Industries, see: U.S. Bureau of the Census, *1987 Census of Service Industries* (Washington: U.S. Census Bureau, November 1989), Tables 1a and 1b.

6. Only facilities with 25 or more beds are included here. See: Genevieve W. Strahan, *Trends in Nursing and Related Care Homes and Hospitals* (Washington: U.S. Department of Health and Human Resources, March 1984).

7. These data are from the *1987 Census of Service Industries.* The Census definition of nursing homes differs slightly from that in the ILTCP and the National Master Facility Inventory (NMFI), as noted earlier. In addition, the 1969-1980 data from the NMFI include only homes with 25 beds or more. Despite these technical differences, the broad trends and differences identified here are still valid.

8. *Health Care Financing Review* (Summer 1990), p. 18.

Education

If health is the largest component of the American nonprofit sector, education is the second largest. One of out every four dollars of nonprofit expenditures are made by nonprofit education institutions, as Figure 2.5 showed. What is more, nonprofit institutions play important roles in all four major segments of the educational system: (1) higher education, (2) elementary and secondary education, (3) vocational education, and (4) library services.

But what exactly is this role, and how does the nonprofit sector compare to government and the for-profit sector in this field?

To answer these questions, this chapter looks first at the basic scale and composition of educational expenditures, and then examines the nonprofit role in each of the major spheres of educational activity.

"Education is the second largest component of the American nonprofit sector."

Education Spending

Overview

Scale. Americans spent $344 billion on education in the 1989 academic year, somewhat less than on health, but still a significant 7 percent of the gross national product.[1]

Sources of spending. Unlike the situation in the health sphere, where private spending is dominant, in education most of the spending originates with government. As of 1989, just over 70 percent of total education spending in the United States came from government, almost 90 percent of it from the state and local level (see Figure 6.1). By comparison, private fees and payments accounted for 25 percent of the total and private philanthropy for about 3 percent.[2]

FIGURE 6.1
Sources of Education Spending, 1989

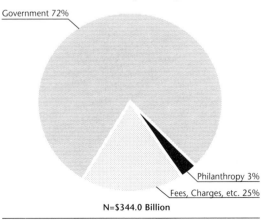

Government 72%

Philanthropy 3%

Fees, Charges, etc. 25%

N=$344.0 Billion

Source: See endnote 1.

FIGURE 6.2
**Growth in Education Institution
Spending, 1975/76–88/89
(Adjusted for Inflation)**

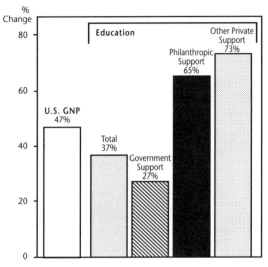

Source: See endnote 2.

FIGURE 6.3
**Government, For Profit, and Nonprofit
Shares of Education Spending, 1987**

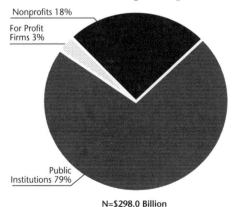

N=$298.0 Billion

Source: See endnote 2.

Recent Trends

Perhaps because of its dependence on government, education spending has not experienced anywhere near as rapid a rate of growth in recent years as has health spending. Thus, while the U.S. gross national product grew by 47 percent in real terms between 1975 and 1989, education spending grew by a much slower 37 percent. As a share of gross national product, therefore, education spending declined from 7.6 percent in 1975 to 7.0 percent by 1989 (see Figure 6.2).

Particularly lagging was government spending, which increased by only 27 percent between 1975 and 1987, or only half as fast as the gross national product as a whole. Faster growth in fees and other charges as well as in philanthropic support helped to boost the growth rate, but these represent much smaller sources of support. The nation's educational institutions have therefore had to adjust to a declining share of the nation's wealth.

The Role of Philanthropy and the Nonprofit Sector

As Figure 6.1 makes clear, philanthropic giving accounts for only about 3 percent of overall education spending in the United States. However, this does not mean that the nonprofit sector as a whole has a limited role in this sphere. To the contrary, compared to the 6 percent share of total gross national product that it absorbs, the nonprofit sector absorbs close to 20 percent of all education expenditures (see Figure 6.3).

Even this fails to do justice to the role that nonprofit organizations play in the education sphere, for in some subfields the nonprofit role is even more significant than this. To see this, it is useful to look in more detail at the four major subfields of education.

Higher Education

The most important of these subfields so far as nonprofit organizations are concerned is higher education. As Figure 6.4 shows, 40 percent of all education spending goes into higher education, a total of almost $136 billion in 1989.[3]

The Nonprofit Role

Institutions. As Figure 6.5 shows, the nonprofit sector plays a very significant role in American higher education. Almost half of all higher education institutions are private nonprofits. Unlike many other countries, whose premier universities are typically government institutions, many of the most distinguished colleges and universities in the United States are private, nonprofit institutions. This includes Harvard, Yale, Princeton, Duke, Stanford, Johns Hopkins, Dartmouth,

Brown, Vanderbilt, Rice, Swarthmore, Williams, Vassar, and many others (see Table 6.1).

Enrollment. Although the private, nonprofit higher education sector contains many large institutions, most private, nonprofit, higher education institutions are smaller than their government counterparts. As a result, although the private institutions represent 49 percent of the institutions, they account for only 20 percent of the students enrolled in higher education, as Figure 6.5 also shows.

Degrees. The nonprofit institutions play a much larger role in the granting of higher education degrees, however. For one thing, many of the public institutions are two-year colleges that do not issue baccalaureate degrees. For another, the nonprofit institutions have traditionally had especially strong graduate and professional programs. As a result, private, nonprofit higher education institutions account for about one-third of all baccalaureate degrees issued in the United States, and just over half of all Ph.D. and professional degrees (e.g., medical degrees, law degrees) (see Figure 6.5).

Expenditures. Reflecting this, nonprofit higher education institutions absorb about one-third of all higher education expenditures (see Figure 6.5). All in all, therefore, they play a much more substantial role than the enrollment figures alone would suggest.

Sources of Funds

The pattern of funding of private higher education institutions differs considerably from that of the public institutions. As Figure 6.6 shows, two-thirds of the revenue of private higher education institutions comes from fees and other sales. Private gifts, grants, contracts, and endowment earnings together account for another 15 percent of support. The balance (20 percent) comes from government. Even for the private institutions, therefore, private philanthropy is only the third most important source of support.

For the public institutions of higher education, government is the dominant source of support. Three out of every five dollars of current fund revenue for the public institutions comes from government. By contrast, fee and sale income accounts for about 40 percent, and private gifts, grants, contracts, and endowment income for about 4 percent.

Recent Trends

The current structure of American higher education is a product of changes that have occurred largely since the Second World War. Prior to this, the nonprofit sector had an even larger role in the higher education

FIGURE 6.4
Where Education Spending Goes, 1989

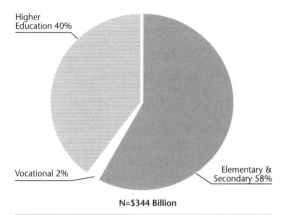

Higher Education 40%

Vocational 2%

Elementary & Secondary 58%

N=$344 Billion

Source: See endnote 2.

FIGURE 6.5
The Nonprofit Role in Higher Education

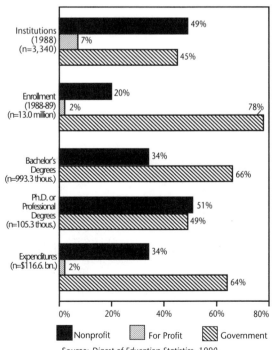

Institutions (1988) (n=3,340): 49%, 7%, 45%

Enrollment (1988-89) (n=13.0 million): 20%, 2%, 78%

Bachelor's Degrees (n=993.3 thous.): 34%, 66%

Ph.D. or Professional Degrees (n=105.3 thous.): 51%, 49%

Expenditures (n=$116.6 bn.): 34%, 2%, 64%

■ Nonprofit ▨ For Profit ▧ Government

Source: *Digest of Education Statistics, 1990,* Tables 3, 157, 164, 217, 278.

TABLE 6.1

Examples of Private Nonprofit Colleges and Universities in the United States

Harvard University
Princeton University
Yale University
Johns Hopkins University
Stanford University
Duke University
Brown University
University of Pennsylvania
Massachusetts Institute of Technology
University of Chicago
Swarthmore College
Vassar College
Smith College
Williams College
Oberlin College

"Nonprofit institutions constitute about half of all higher education institutions and just over half of all advanced degrees."

sphere than it does now. As late as 1950, for example, almost two-thirds of all higher education institutions were private nonprofits, and these institutions held half of all the higher-education students.[4]

Beginning in the 1950s, and accelerating in the 1960s, however, state and local governments made major investments to build comprehensive systems of public higher education, embracing both two- and four-year institutions. As a consequence, enrollment in American higher education increased dramatically—by 40 percent in the 1950s, and by another 120 percent in the 1960s. Public higher education naturally claimed the lion's share of this increase, increasing its enrollments by 60 percent in the 1950s and 170 percent in the 1960s. By 1980, therefore, close to 80 percent of all students enrolled in higher education in the United States were in public institutions compared to 20 percent in private ones.

Since 1980, however, changes in higher education have been far less dramatic. After three decades of rapid growth, the growth rate of public higher education has slowed considerably, restrained particularly by pressures on government budgets. Between 1980 and 1989, the expenditures of higher education institutions grew by 45 percent overall. Significantly, private institutions did slightly better than public ones during this decade, boosting their expenditures by 49 percent compared to 41 percent for the public institutions (see Figure 6.7). Most of this increased revenue came from increased tuitions and fees for services, however, not charitable giving or government support.

The slowdown in the growth of higher education is even more evident in figures on the growth in enrollments and in the number of institutions. As Figure 6.7 shows, the number of higher education institutions grew by just 4 percent during the 1980s, and the num-

FIGURE 6.6

Sources of Current Fund Revenue of Public and Private Higher Education Institutions, 1987

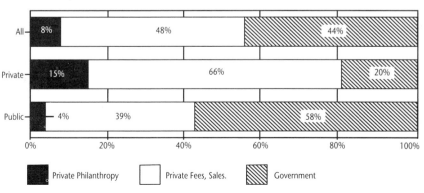

Source: *Digest of Education Statistics*, (1990) Tables 291, 292, 293, pp. 294–296.

ber of students enrolled grew by just 8 percent. Growth was limited among both the public and non-profit institutions, moreover. The one dynamic element in the picture has been the growth of the for-profit sector in the higher education field. About half of the new higher education institutions created in the 1980s were for-profits, mostly technical and vocational schools, and the for- profit sector accounted for over 10 percent of the growth in enrollment in higher education that occurred during this period (compared to its 2 percent share of all students enrolled.) In other words, having confronted a major challenge from public higher education institutions during the 1960s and 1970s, private, nonprofit higher education institutions may be poised for a challenge from for-profit institutions in the 1990s.

Elementary and Secondary Education

Overview
While nonprofit institutions have traditionally provided most of the higher education in the United States, public institutions have been the dominant force at the elementary and secondary level, at least since the latter nineteenth century. Elementary and secondary education absorbs about 60 percent of all education spending as Figure 6.4 noted, and government provided over 90 percent of this.

Government and Nonprofit Roles

The government presence. Not only is government the chief funder of elementary and secondary education; it is also the chief *provider* of it, a situation that is different from what prevails in most other domestic fields. Thus, as shown in Figure 6.8, as of 1988, public schools accounted for 76 percent of all elementary and secondary school institutions, 89 percent of all elementary and secondary school pupils, and 92 percent of all elementary and secondary school expenditures.

Nonprofit role. This is not to say that the nonprofit sector does not have an important role even at the elementary and secondary education level. As of 1988, there were close to 27,000 private, nonprofit elementary and secondary schools in the United States. One out of every four elementary and secondary schools, therefore, is a nonprofit. These schools enrolled 5.2 million students, or more than one out of every 10 students in school. In some sections of the country, moreover, this proportion is considerably higher. In Pennsylvania, for example, close to 20 percent of the students are in private, nonprofit elementary and secondary schools. In Wisconsin, the proportion is 17

"One out or every four elementary and secondary schools is a nonprofit."

FIGURE 6.7
Recent Higher Education Trends

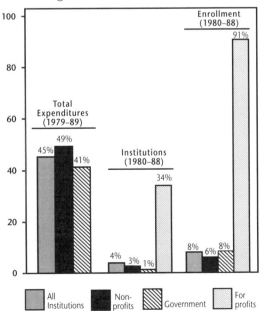

Source: Author's calculations based on data in *Digest of Education Statistics, 1990*, Tables 3, 217, 164, 28.

FIGURE 6.8
Nonprofit Share of Elementary and Secondary Education

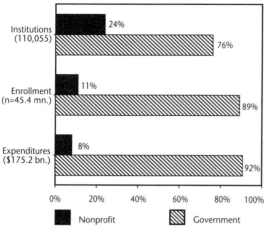

Source: *Digest of Educational Statistics*, (1990), Tables 5, 3, 29.

FIGURE 6.9
Recent Trends in Elementary and Secondary Education

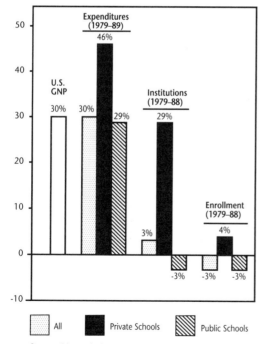

Source: *Digest of Educational Statistics*, (1990), Tables 5, 3, 29.

percent, and in Illinois and Connecticut, it is 15 percent.[5] Generally speaking, the proportion of students in private schools is lowest in the South and the West, and highest in the Northeast and Midwest.

Religious affiliation. One reason for this pattern is the close connection between religion and private elementary and secondary education. Just over half of all students enrolled in private elementary and secondary schools are enrolled in Catholic schools. The areas of the country with large Catholic populations thus tend to have the largest concentrations of private elementary and secondary schools. Another 30 percent of the students enrolled in private elementary and secondary schools are in schools with some other religious affiliation. Well over 80 percent of the students in private elementary and secondary schools are therefore enrolled in schools with an explicit religious affiliation.

Recent Trends
Not only have private, nonprofit organizations retained an important foothold in the elementary and secondary education field, but also that foothold has been growing. During the past 30 years, a significant consolidation has been under way in public elementary and secondary education. The number of public schools thus declined from almost 120,000 in 1959 to just under 85,000 in 1987.[6] Although enrollments continued to grow, the end of the "baby boom" kept that growth constrained.

Because some of these changes have been dictated by demographic realities, they have affected private schools as well as public ones. However, in more recent years there is evidence that the private sector is gaining ground on the public one in this field. Thus, as Figure 6.9 shows, the expenditures of private elementary and secondary schools grew more rapidly during the 1980s than did those of the public schools (46 percent vs. 29 percent). Over 6,000 net, new private schools were added during this period, while the number of public schools continued to decline. Finally, while overall elementary and secondary school enrollment declined, private elementary and secondary schools registered an increase of 4 percent, mostly at the kindergarten to eighth-grade level.

Several factors may be responsible for this interesting trend. One is almost certainly the rise of the religious fundamentalist movement and the move to create religiously affiliated elementary and secondary schools. A second is dissatisfaction with inner-city public schools, which has prompted residents in many areas to turn to private schools instead. Whatever the source, this trend provides further evidence of the value of the nonprofit sector as a "safety valve" to absorb demands for change and provide alternative ways to respond to human needs.

Vocational Education

Overview

In addition to the formal, academic institutions discussed earlier, nonprofit organizations also play a significant role in the provision of vocational education through correspondence and trade schools, such as data processing schools, business and secretarial schools, commercial arts schools, practical nursing schools, and drama and music schools.[7] Data on public sector activity in this arena is limited, but information on the private sector involvement make it clear that this has become a substantial $6.2 billion industry.

Nonprofit and For-Profit Roles

For-profit dominance. As Figure 6.10 makes clear, for-profit firms are clearly the dominant element in this industry. As of 1987, such firms constituted 76 percent of the establishments, received 78 percent of the revenues, and employed 75 percent of the staff.

Nonprofit involvement. Nevertheless, nonprofit organizations maintain a significant presence in this field. Thus, between a fifth and a quarter of all vocational education activity relies on nonprofit organizations.

Recent Trends

Overall growth. This type of nonacademic vocational training has grown quite dramatically in recent years. As Figure 6.11 makes clear, between 1977 and 1987, the revenues of private providers of vocational education increased by 84 percent after adjusting for inflation. During this same period, overall gross national product increased by about 27 percent.

For-profit expansion. For-profit providers were clearly the dominant element in this growth. Between 1977 and 1987, the number of for-profit firms providing such specialized vocational training increased by 58 percent, the number of employees in the for-profit branch of the industry increased by 80 percent, and the revenues jumped by 98 percent, even after adjusting for inflation. The comparable changes for nonprofits, as Figure 6.11 makes clear, were much smaller. In other words, for-profit firms are managing to eke out a niche for themselves in the educational field, where government and nonprofit organizations have heretofore held the dominant position. At the same

FIGURE 6.10
The Nonprofit Role in Vocational Education, 1987

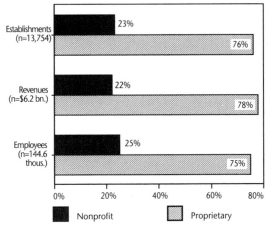

Source: *1987 Census of Service Industries,* (1989), Tables 1a, 1b.

FIGURE 6.11
Recent Trends in Private Vocational Training, 1977–1987

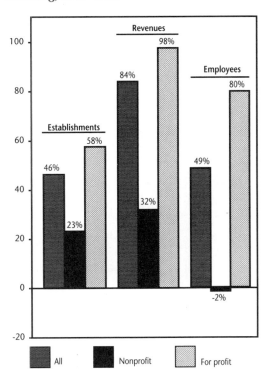

Source: *Census of Service Industries,* (1987), Tables 1a, 1b; (1977), Tables 1, 2.

time, even in this area of considerable for-profit growth, nonprofits maintain an important position.

Libraries

One final aspect of education worth exploring is the provision of library services. To a significant extent, such services have already been covered in our earlier discussion of higher education and elementary education, because most higher education and secondary schools have their own school libraries.

However, there are also more than 10,000 free-standing libraries.[8] Most of these (85 percent) are public institutions, reflecting the same philosophy that motivated the creation of the system of public elementary and secondary education—the desire to improve the general educational level of the population. Like public education, moreover, these libraries are almost all run by local governments, although a limited amount of federal support is available to them. They therefore have a considerable amount of autonomy and local control.

Beyond these public libraries and school libraries, however, there are also some 1,400 private, nonprofit libraries in the United States employing over 13,000 people and receiving some $38 million in revenue.[9] These private, nonprofit libraries constitute 14 percent of all the nonschool libraries. If the private college and university libraries were included, it is probably reasonable to conclude that nonprofit organizations operate at least a third of all adult libraries in the United States.

Conclusion

Public schools have long been the predominant providers of education at the elementary and secondary levels in the United States, while private institutions have historically had a major role at the college and university level.

During the past several decades, however, public institutions have expanded rapidly at the higher education level in response to growing public demand for education in the aftermath of World War II. As a result, they now constitute almost half of the institutions and enroll the preponderance of students at the higher education level as well.

Nevertheless, private nonprofit institutions retain an important foothold in the education field. Not only do they account for nearly half of the higher education institutions, but also they account for at least a third of the enrollments and expenditures and slightly over half of the advanced degrees. What is more, they play a significant, and recently growing, role at the elementary and secondary level as well.

"Nonprofit organizations operate at least a third of all adult libraries in the United States."

"One out of every five education dollars is used to purchase educational services from a nonprofit provider."

Thus, nonprofit organizations are a pivotal part of the American educational system, just as they are of the American health system, with a reputation for quality and independence that helps them provide—both at the elementary and secondary level and at the higher education level—an important measure of diversity and choice.

ENDNOTES

1. The principal source of these data on educational spending is the *Digest of Education Statistics, 1990* (Washington, DC: National Center for Education Statistics, February 1991), Table 28, p. 33. However, the *Digest* excludes noncollegiate, postsecondary institutions. Data on these were obtained from the 1987 and 1977 *Census of Service Industries*, Tables 1a and 1b, and were projected to 1988/89. Data reported here represent expenditures of education institutions and therefore include research and other noneducational expenditures.

2. Data on sources of support of elementary, secondary, and higher education from *Digest of Education Statistics, 1990*, Table 29, p. 34; total income of vocational education institutions from *1987 Census of Service Industries*, Tables 1a and 1b; data on government support of vocational education from *Social Security Bulletin* (February 1990), p. 18; balance of vocational support assumed to come from fees and charges; data on philanthropic giving to education from *Giving USA* 1988, p. 89. Figures for government spending here may differ from those presented earlier because the earlier figures, developed by the Social Security Administration, cover education only, whereas these data cover all income of educational institutions including, for example, research income.

3. Higher education includes study beyond secondary school at an institution that offers programs terminating in an associate, baccalaureate, or higher degree. Not included is study at a noncollegiate, vocational institution. *Digest of Education Statistics, 1990*, p. 441.

4. *Digest of Education Statistics, 1990*, Table 3, p. 12; and Table 216, p. 228.

5. *Digest of Education Statistics, 1990*, Tables 37 and 57, pp. 50 and 71.

6. *Digest of Education Statistics, 1990*, Tables 84 and 5, pp. 96 and 14.

7. This category includes those establishments classified under Standard Industrial Classification (SIC) codes 824 and 829—"Vocational schools" and "Schools and educational services not elsewhere classified." See *1987 Census of Service Industries*, p. a-17.

8. This figure is derived by adding together the 8,597 public library systems identified in the *Digest of Education Statistics*, 1990, Table 376, p. 395, and the 1,570 private libraries identified in the *1987 U.S. Census of Service Industries*, Tables 1a and 1b. The public figure is for 1982 and excludes branches.

"Nonprofit organizations play important roles in all four major segments of the American educational system: (1) higher education, (2) elementary and secondary education, (3) vocational education, and (4) library services."

9. In addition to the private nonprofit libraries, there are 178 private for-profit libraries identified in the U.S. Census of Service Industries for 1987. See: *U.S. Census of Service Industries*, 1987, Table 1a and 1b. SIC code 823 includes "establishments primarily engaged in providing library services, including the circulation of books and other materials for reading, study, and reference."

CHAPTER SEVEN

Social Services

For all their complexity, the fields of health and education are still generally comprehensible to most people. Although there may be uncertainties over the precise definition of an "outpatient clinic," there are few people who do not have some clear idea of what a hospital or a university is.

Not so with the third major field of nonprofit activity: social services. The term itself is ambiguous, and the range of organizations typically grouped under it exceedingly diverse.

Yet, more people probably have contact with nonprofit social service agencies than with any other type, if for no other reason than that they are so numerous. In fact, as Chapter 2 made clear, there are more nonprofit public-benefit social service organizations than any other kind—63,000 agencies as of 1987 compared to only 3,400 nonprofit hospitals, 4,100 nonprofit nursing homes, and 3,300 nonprofit colleges and universities. In addition, there are many thousand more "mutual benefit organizations"—informal self-help groups, many with few or no paid staff.

What do these organizations do? What is the "social services" field, and what role do nonprofit organizations play in it? How has this role changed in recent years in view of the significant government spending cutbacks that have occurred? This chapter seeks to answer these questions.

The Social Service Field

Definition

Although the term social services is somewhat amorphous, the basic concept behind it is fairly straightforward. Social services are essentially forms of assistance, other than outright cash aid, that help indi-

"'Social services' are forms of assistance, other than outright cash aid, that allow individuals and families to function in the face of social, economic, and physical problems or that provide assistance that families or neighbors once provided informally."

"While the largest single source of funding for social services is government, the major providers of the services are private, nonprofit organizations."

FIGURE 7.1
Spending on Social Services vs. Health and Education, 1987*

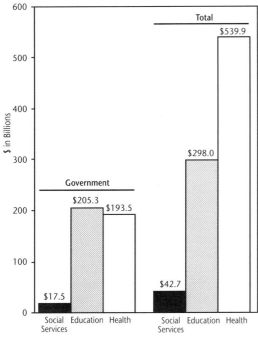

Source: See endnotes 1 and 2.
*Health figure is for 1988.

FIGURE 7.2
Sources of Social Services Spending, 1987

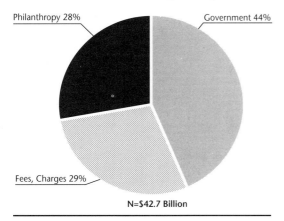

N=$42.7 Billion

Source: See endnote 2.

viduals and families to function in the face of social, economic, or physical problems, or that provide assistance that families or neighbors once provided informally. Included are day-care services, adoption assistance, family counseling, residential care for individuals who cannot function on their own (e.g., the elderly or the physically or mentally handicapped), vocational rehabilitation, disaster assistance, refugee assistance, emergency food assistance, substance abuse treatment, neighborhood improvement, and many more.

Overall Scale
The social services field has expanded greatly in recent decades as a result of two interrelated developments: first, economic and demographic changes that have expanded the need for such services (e.g., the aging of the population, which has increased the need for elderly feeding and home health services, and the increased entry of women into the workforce, which has expanded the need for child day care); and second, increased government funding, especially since the early 1960s, which has made it easier to meet this expanded need.

The scale of social service spending barely compares with that of health or education, however. Of the $834 billion in government social welfare spending in 1987, only $17.5 billion, or about 2 percent, went for social services.[1] With private spending included, total social service spending naturally exceeds this amount, but still falls far short of the spending on health or education. Thus, as of 1987, total social service spending totalled approximately $43 billion, or about four-tenths of 1 percent of the U.S. gross national product. By comparison, health spending totalled $540 billion and education spending almost $300 billion (see Figure 7.1).[2]

Sources of Social Service Spending
As shown in Figure 7.2, government is the largest single source of social service spending in the United States. Forty-four percent of this spending came from government as of 1987 despite nearly a decade of retrenchment. Of the remaining spending, about 29 percent came from service charges and fees and 27 percent from private philanthropic giving.

Self-Help and Mutual Assistance
In addition to the more formal, organized provision of social services, there is a vast quantity of informal assistance of a similar sort that is provided through self-help groups. Some of these groups are highly structured, such as Alcoholics Anonymous. But others

are much more informal and unstructured, consisting of individuals and families who share a common experience, such as loss of a child or the presence of a handicap, and who meet together for mutual support. The National Institute of Mental Health identifies three distinct types of such groups: first, groups for people with a physical or mental illness; second, recovery groups for people with problems such as alcoholism, drug addiction or the like; and, third, groups for certain minorities, such as the handicapped. As many as half a million such groups are estimated to exist in the United States.[3]

Nonprofit, Government, and For-Profit Roles

While government is the largest single source of social service funding, however, private, nonprofit organizations are the major providers of the services. At the same time, government agencies and for-profit providers also play important roles.

The Nonprofit Role

Overall role. As noted earlier, there were approximately 63,000 nonprofit organizations providing social services in the United States as of 1987. Of these, the most numerous were providers of *individual and family services* (35 percent) and *child day care* (22 percent), as shown in Figure 7.3. The rest provided *residential care* (17 percent), *job training* (8 percent), and assorted other social services.[4] In financial terms, residential care ranks higher with 22 percent of the total revenues, reflecting the relatively large size of most residential care facilities. Day care, by contrast, ranks lower, with only 14 percent of the revenues.[5]

The significant role of the nonprofit sector in the provision of social services is evident in Figure 7.4. As this figure shows, nonprofit organizations account for:

- 59 percent of the private social service agencies.[6]
- 74 percent of all social service revenues.[7]
- 58 percent of all social service agency employment—an estimated 1.1 million employees in all.[8]

In addition, nonprofit social service organizations also engage the energies of a sizable army of volunteers. According to recent estimates, these volunteers contribute time that is equivalent to another 800,000 full-time employees in addition to the estimated 1.1 million paid employees of these agencies.[9]

Variations by subfield. Although nonprofit organizations play a major role in all facets of the social service field, there are significant variations among the subfields. As shown in Figure 7.5, among private social

FIGURE 7.3
Types of Nonprofit Social Service Agencies, 1987

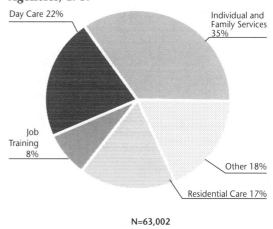

N=63,002

Source: *1987 Census of Service Industries.*

service agencies, nonprofits comprise:

- 83 percent of the individual and family services agencies.
- 74 percent of the vocational rehabilitation agencies.
- 55 percent of the residential care facilities.
- 89 percent of the other social service providers.

In only one subfield (day care) does the nonprofit share of the total drop below half.

This picture of substantial nonprofit involvement would be even more dramatic if we were to focus on revenues instead of numbers of agencies because non-profit providers tend to be larger than their for-profit counterparts. Thus, the nonprofit share of the revenues of private social service agencies totals:

- 92 percent in the case of individual and family services.
- 82 percent in the case of job training and vocational rehabilitation.
- 71 percent in the case of residential care.
- 96 percent in the case of other social services.
- 43 percent in the case of day care.

In short, the nonprofit sector plays an immense role in the provision of social services.

Government agencies

Although nonprofit organizations are the major providers of social services, government agencies also play a significant role in this field. As we have seen, government is the principal financier of social services. But government agencies also help to deliver certain kinds of social services, even though most gov-ernment-funded services are delivered by others. Thus, some 400,000 government employees are engaged in various "public welfare" activities. Most of these manage the cash assistance programs (e.g., Aid to Families with Dependent Children, and general assistance) at the local level, provide "casework" to client families, and oversee contractual arrangements with private providers to deliver social services to tar-get populations. Public employees also manage the foster care system that places children without suit-able homes in foster care settings. Altogether, about 23 percent of the employees in the social service/pub-lic welfare field work for government agencies—a sig-nificant proportion, but well below what the level of public spending in this field might suggest.

For-Profit Providers

One of the more important developments in the social service field in recent years has been the emer-

FIGURE 7.4
The Nonprofit Role in Social Services, 1987

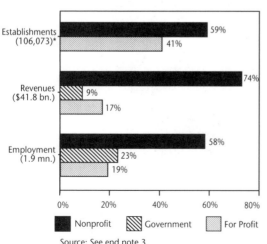

Source: See end note 3.
*Includes private agencies only.

gence of a for-profit sector within it. Although for-profit firms still play a relatively small role in this field, they accounted as of 1987 for 17 percent of the social-service revenues, 19 percent of the employment, and 41 percent of the nongovernmental establishments, as Figure 7.4 shows.

In some fields, moreover, the for-profit presence is considerably larger than this. Thus, as Figure 7.5 shows, for-profit organizations constitute two-thirds of the day-care agencies and 45 percent of the residential care facilities. They also absorb 57 percent and 29 percent, respectively, of the revenues in these fields.

Unlike the nonprofit providers, the for-profit ones tend to rely more heavily on fees and service charges to support their activities. This reflects the growth in demand for social services throughout the population. Once heavily focused on the poor, the social services field has expanded considerably, creating a market for for-profit providers.

"One of the more important developments in the social services field in recent years has been the emergence of a for-profit sector within it."

Recent Trends

The emergence of a sizable for-profit sector in the social services field is but a part of a broader set of changes that has affected this field over the past decade or more. Broadly speaking, these changes can be grouped under three major headings.

Declining Governmental Role

Perhaps the dominant development of the decade of the 1980s in the field of social services was the sharp reversal that occurred in the previous pattern of growth in government activity. From the mid-1960s to the late 1970s, a major expansion of government involvement took place, as efforts were made to com-

FIGURE 7.5
Nonprofit vs. For Profit Providers of Social Services, by Subfield

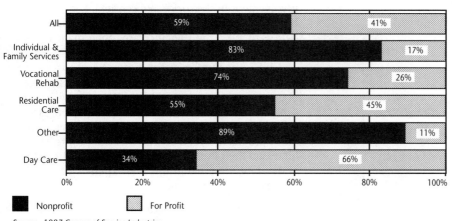

Source: *1987 Census of Service Industries.*

FIGURE 7.6
Key Trends in Social Services, 1977–1987

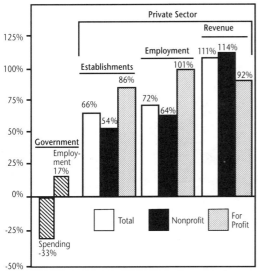

Source: See endnote 10.

"...between 1977 and 1987, the number of for-profit social service establishments increased by 86 percent."

bat persistent poverty by providing a variety of supportive services to individuals and families and, thus, increase the opportunities available to them to enter the workforce.

As Figure 7.6 makes clear, however, in real, inflation-adjusted terms, that growth essentially stopped in the 1980s and reversed course. Thus, between 1977 and 1987, the real value of government spending for social services declined by 33 percent. Government employment in this field continued to grow, but quite slowly, with only 66,000 new employees added despite efforts to intensify administration of many of the basic public assistance programs.

Overall Growth

Despite the reduction in government support, however, considerable growth nevertheless occurred in the social services field during the 1980s. Thus, as Figure 7.6 also makes clear, between 1977 and 1987:

- The number of private social service *agencies* recorded by the Census of Service Industries grew by 66 percent.
- The number of *employees* working for these agencies grew by 72 percent.
- The *revenues* these agencies collected expanded by 111 percent after adjusting for inflation.[10]

Marketization

How can we explain this apparent paradox of continued growth despite the loss of the principal source of income in this field? The answer seems to be a significant shift in the character of the social services field in the direction of what might be termed *marketization*, that is, the penetration of the market into the field. This took place in two principal ways.

Growth of for-profit firms. In the first place, as we have seen, there was considerable growth in for-profit involvement in the social services field. For profits had already gained a considerable foothold in this field as of 1977, but they increased their market share considerably during the 1980s. Thus, between 1977 and 1987, the number of for-profit social service establishments increased by 86 percent, the number of employees in these establishments grew by 101 percent, and the revenues expanded by 92 percent (see Figure 7.6). Except for revenues, the growth of nonprofit providers lagged behind this. For profits increased their involvement particularly in the fields of day-care and job training, and experienced considerable growth as well in residential care.

Increased reliance on fee income. That for profits

were able to increase their market share in the social service field at a time of declining government involvement was due in large part to a second aspect of the marketization of this field: the growth of fee-for-service activity. Between 1977 and 1987, the fee share of social service agency income grew from an estimated 11 percent to 29 percent.[11]

Much of this growth accrued, naturally enough, to the for-profit social service providers. But nonprofit providers benefited as well. A little under a quarter of the growth in nonprofit social service agency income between 1977 and 1987 came from fees for service, even though such fees constituted only 9 percent of total income when the period began. In addition, other business income contributed another 11 percent. About 35 percent of the increase in income of nonprofit human service organizations between 1977 and 1987 thus came from essentially commercial sources. Although private giving to these organizations also grew considerably, the growth in this commercial income was especially striking, doubling between 1977 and 1987 as a share of nonprofit social service agency income.

"Over one-third of the increase in income of nonprofit social service organizations between 1977 and 1987 came from essentially commercial sources."

Conclusion

The social services field is thus a true mixed economy, with active involvement on the part of nonprofit, government, and for-profit agencies, and extensive support from government revenues, fee income, and private philanthropy. As a general rule, however, private nonprofit agencies dominate the delivery of social services, and government sources dominate the funding of them. It is this partnership that has formed the heart of the human service delivery system of the nation for the past three decades.

During the 1980s, however, a significant disruption occurred in this established pattern, as government support dwindled considerably. Social service agencies seem to have weathered this storm, largely by moving social services increasingly into the market system. A significant growth also occurred in private giving in this field, but the really dynamic element appears to have been the growth of commercial forces.

ENDNOTES

1. Included here is spending on social services under the basic public assistance programs (Title IV of the Social Security Act), vocational rehabilitation, child welfare, Office of Economic Opportunity and Action programs, "other public aid" under public assistance (including work relief, other emergency aid, surplus food for the

needy, temporary employment assistance, and work-experience training), and "social welfare not elsewhere classified." *Social Security Bulletin*, Vol. 53, No. 2 (February 1990), pp. 18-19; *Social Security Bulletin*, Vol. 54, No. 10 (November 1991); and unpublished Social Security administration data.

2. Data on health spending from *Health Care Financing Review*, Vol. 11, No. 4 (Summer 1990), Table 15, p. 30. Data on education spending from *Digest of Education Statistics*, 1990, Table 29, p. 34 and *1987 Census of Service Industries*. No data series comparable to that for education and health spending is available on social services spending. The estimate of social service spending reported here was therefore constructed by adding together data on revenues of nonprofit and for-profit social service organizations provided in the *1987 Census of Service Industries* with an estimate of the revenues of the direct government social service providers. The latter was developed by subtracting from total government social service expenditures the amount of government support to nonprofit social services agencies reported in *Dimensions of the Independent Sector*, 1989, p. 177, and an estimate of government support to for-profit social service providers. The latter was calculated assuming that for-profit providers received proportionally half as much government support as their size in relation to nonprofit providers might suggest.

3. U.S. Department of Health and Human Services, Public Health Service, *Surgeon General's Workshop on Self-Help and Public Health* (Washington, DC: U.S. Government Printing Office, 1988), p. 1.

4. Based on data in *1987 Census of Service Industries*. These divisions are naturally somewhat arbitrary because many organizations perform a variety of functions. This is particularly true of the generally large "individual and family services" agencies.

5. Job training is close in size to residential care, with 21 percent of the revenues. The remaining category, social services not elsewhere classified, accounts for 15 percent of the revenues. From *1987 Census of Service Industries*.

6. An indeterminate number of government social service agencies also exist. Most cities, counties, and state governments have such offices. This means that there are probably 5,000 such government institutions, although they are typically parts of state and local government and not separate organizations.

7. Nonprofit and for-profit revenue data are from *1987 Census of Service Industries*. The derivation of the revenues of government social service providers is provided in endnote 2.

8. Data on for-profit and nonprofit employment come from *1987 Census of Service Industries*. Data on government employment are from *Statistical Abstract of the U.S. 1990*, p. 300, and are based on U.S. Bureau of the Census, *Public Employment in 1987*, series GE 87, No. 1. Government employment includes all "public welfare" and is therefore probably overstated because it includes employees involved in the administration of the basic public welfare programs in addition to those providing social services.

9. Hodgkinson, Weizman, et. al. *Nonprofit Almanac* (1989), p. 43.

10. Data on government spending are from *Social Security Bulletin*, Vol. 46, No. 8 (August 1983, p. 10, and Vol. 53, No. 2 (February 1990), pp. 18-19. Data on government employment in public welfare are from *U.S. Statistical Abstract, 1990 and 1980*. Data private establishments, employment, and revenues are from *U.S. Census of Service Industries* (1977) and (1987). Estimates of revenue growth are probably overstated because 1977 data refer to expenditures only and 1987 data include all revenues.

11. Author's estimates based on data identified in endnote 2.

CHAPTER EIGHT

Arts, Culture and Recreation

In addition to the role they play in the delivery of health, education, and welfare services, nonprofit organizations also play a major role in the artistic, cultural, and recreational life of the United States. This role can easily be overlooked, however, because arts and culture organizations comprise a relatively small part of the entire nonprofit sector (only 3 percent of the organizations and 2 percent of the expenditures), and because nonprofits tend to be prominent only in a relatively small portion of the arts and recreation field. Yet the importance of the nonprofit sector in this field goes well beyond what numbers alone might suggest. Indeed, most of the serious cultural and artistic activity of the nation takes place in nonprofit organizations.

Overview: Culture and Recreation in the United States

Americans devote almost 8 percent of their total consumption expenditures to recreation, a figure that has been rising steadily over the past several decades.[1] Included here are purchases of recreational products such as books, sporting goods, toys, and televisions, as well as involvement in recreational services.

The recreational services portion of the recreation and culture field itself employs over 1.6 million people. Of these, the vast majority (90 percent) are involved in sports and recreation activities, including 21 percent in motion picture-related services and 69 percent in sports and other recreation. This leaves about 10 percent, some 166,000 people in all, who are involved in what can more narrowly be termed arts and culture, including theater, music, museums, art galleries, and the like (see Figure 8.1).[2]

"...most of the serious cultural and artistic activity of the nation takes place in nonprofit organizations."

FIGURE 8.1
Employment in Arts and Recreational Services, 1987

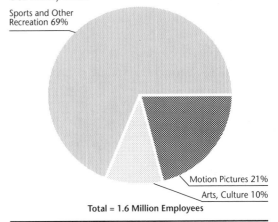

Sports and Other Recreation 69%

Motion Pictures 21%

Arts, Culture 10%

Total = 1.6 Million Employees

Source: See endnote 2.

The Nonprofit Role in Recreation and Arts

Nonprofit organizations are involved in both the sports/recreation and the arts and culture segments of this field. As with the other types of providers, most nonprofit activity is in the sports and recreation area. But it is in arts and culture where nonprofits play their most distinctive and significant role.

Nature and Extent of Nonprofit Activity

As Table 8.1 shows, there were nearly 13,000 nonprofit organizations involved in the provision of cultural and recreational services as of 1987, the latest date for which information is available. These organizations employed at least 236,000 people and had revenues of almost $10 billion.[3]

Of these nearly 13,000 organizations, most (57 percent) are *sports and recreation clubs*. These clubs account for 54 percent of the nonprofit arts and recreation organization employees and 42 percent of the revenues. By comparison, only about 40 percent of the nonprofit arts and recreation organizations are involved in *arts and culture* per se, including theatrical production companies, orchestras and other musical entertainment institutions, and museums and art galleries. These cultural organizations accounted for 46 percent of the nonprofit employment in this field and 45 percent of the revenues. Another 5 percent of the organizations are public radio and television stations, which are organized locally as nonprofit organizations. These stations account for 13 percent of the nonprofit revenues in this field.

Nonprofit versus For-profit and Government Roles
For-profit dominance in sports and recreation.
While most nonprofit cultural and recreational orga-

"Most nonprofit recreation and arts activity is in the sports and recreation part of the field. But it is in arts and culture where nonprofits play their most distinctive and significant role."

TABLE 8.1

Nonprofit Culture and Recreation Organizations, by Type, 1987

Type	Establishments		Employees		Revenues ($bn)	
	Number	%	Number	%	Amount	%
Theater	1,151	9%	22.7	10%	$0.8	8%
Bands, orchestras, other entertainers	981	8	33.8	14	1.0	10
Museums, art galleries, zoos	2,695	21	52.1	22	2.6	27
Subtotal, arts and culture	4,827	38%	108.6	46%	$4.4	45%
Sports and recreation clubs, fairs	7,218	57	127.5	54	4.1	42
Public radio and television stations	622	5	N.A.	N.A.	1.3	13
Total	12,667	100%	236.1	100%	$9.8	100%

Source: Public radio and television from *Statistical Abstract of the U.S.*, (1990), p. 553; all others from 1987 *Census of Service Industries*.

nizations are in the sports and recreation portion of this field, they are not the dominant force there. Rather, the public and for-profit sectors play a far more significant role as providers of sports and recreational services. Thus, 84 percent of the *private* employment in sports and recreation is in the for-profit sector, and considerable numbers of government employees are involved in this field as well.

Nonprofit dominance in arts and culture. Although smaller in absolute numbers, however, the nonprofit role in the arts and culture portion of the entertainment field is far more important in relative terms, as Figure 8.2 shows. In particular:

Theater. At least 40 percent of the theatrical production and related theatrical services companies in the United States are nonprofits, and they account for just over half of the theatrical services employment.[4] Many live theatrical production companies are for-profit businesses, particularly in the major cultural centers such as New York. But outside of New York and a few other cultural centers, most theaters are nonprofit organizations. These nonprofit theaters provide a critical proving ground for new plays and approaches and help to ensure the survival of theater outside the major production centers.

Orchestras and other entertainment. Well over 90 percent of the orchestras, opera companies, and chamber music groups in the country are nonprofit organizations, and these organizations account for 97 percent of the employment in this field. For-profit firms are the dominant element in other aspects of the music and entertainment field (e.g., music and entertainment groups and the recording industry), but in the field of live classical music, the nonprofit sector holds virtually unrivalled sway. This situation differs markedly from that in Europe and elsewhere in the world, where government involvement is far more substantial.

Museums, art galleries, and botanical and zoological gardens. Nonprofits are nearly as prominent among museums, art galleries, and zoological gardens. Seventy-one percent of these institutions are nonprofits, and they account for the lion's share of the employment.[5]

The Role of Private Philanthropy
Although nonprofit organizations play a major role in the arts and culture field, this does not mean that private charitable support is the principal source of support for this role. To be sure, of the total revenues of nonprofit arts and culture organizations, 63 percent

FIGURE 8.2
The Nonprofit Share of Arts and Culture Establishments and Employment

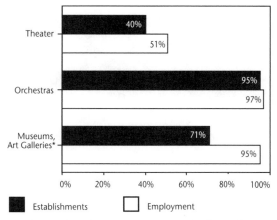

*Employment data relate to private museums and galleries only.
Source: *1987 Census of Service Industries.*

"Although nonprofit organizations play a major role in the arts and culture field, this does not mean that private charitable support is the principal source of support for this role."

FIGURE 8.3
Sources of Nonprofit Arts and Entertainment Organization Operating Income, 1989

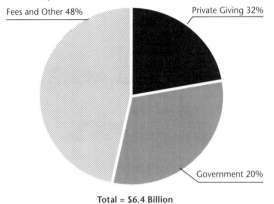

Fees and Other 48%

Private Giving 32%

Government 20%

Total = $6.4 Billion

Source: See endnote 6.

"...unlike most of the other fields we have examined, in arts and culture nonprofit organizations performed better than for-profit organizations during the turbulent decade of the 1980s."

came from private philanthropy as of 1989. However, this includes the value of donated works of art (at current market value) and contributions to endowment and capital funds. If we focus only on general operating support, that is, the funds these institutions use in a given year for salaries, upkeep, and related costs, then private charitable support accounts for a considerably smaller 32 percent of the total (see Figure 8.3). By contrast, fees and other income comprised 48 percent, and government comprised 20 percent.[6]

Recent Trends

Perhaps because government support was so limited to start with, nonprofit arts and culture organizations did fairly well during the 1980s, when government support was falling so sharply. Indeed, unlike most of the other fields we have examined, in arts and culture nonprofit organizations performed better than for-profit organizations.

Overall Growth

This point is evident in Figure 8.4, which records changes in the employment of nonprofit and for-profit organizations in the three fields where nonprofits are particularly important—theater; symphonic and chamber music and opera; and museums, art galleries, and zoos. As Figure 8.4 shows, at a time when overall spending on recreation was increasing by 50 percent in inflation-adjusted terms, nonprofit theaters boosted their employment by 161 percent, nonprofit orchestras and operas boosted their employment by 83 percent, and nonprofit museums, art galleries, and zoos increased their employment by 138 percent. The comparable figures for for-profit establishments in these same fields were 46 percent, 25 percent, and -26 percent, that is, at best only about a fourth as large. In other words, for-profit establishments were either growing much more slowly or actually shrinking.[7]

Sources of Nonprofit Growth

Two sources seem to have been principally responsible for this growth of nonprofit cultural institutions. The first is fees and other earned income. Approximately 46 percent of the growth in nonprofit arts and culture organization *operating* income between 1977 and 1987 came from this source. As a consequence, fee income grew as a share of total nonprofit cultural-institution income.

In addition, however, private giving also grew robustly. About 42 percent of the real, inflation-adjusted growth in nonprofit arts and culture organization operating income between 1977 and 1987 came from this source. By contrast, only about 12 percent of the growth in operating support seems to have come from government. Unlike some of the other fields, where private giving fell behind as a share of income in the face of government retrenchment, therefore, in the arts and culture field, private giving held its own and even gained ground somewhat as a share of income. Even so, it ended the period still behind fees and other earned income as a source of support.

Conclusions

Nonprofit organizations thus play a critical role in the cultural and artistic life of the United States. Although the recreation and entertainment industry as a whole is dominated by for-profit providers, non-profit organizations are clearly the primary producers of live cultural entertainment—theater, symphonic music, opera, and galleries and museums.

Despite the pressures of the 1980s, moreover, the nonprofit position in this field seems quite secure. In fact, nonprofit providers managed to register impressive growth. In part this was due to the generosity of private benefactors. But in somewhat greater part, it was due to the willingness of patrons to pay for the services they received.

ENDNOTES

1. The exact figure is 7.7 percent as of 1989. As recently as 1980, this figure stood at 6.6 percent. From *Statistical Abstract of the United States*, 1991, p. 231.

2. Data on for-profit and nonprofit employment in entertainment and recreational services from *1987 Census of Service Industries*, Tables 1a and 1b. Data on government employment covers employment in "parks and recreation" from U.S. Bureau of the Census, *Public Employment in 1987*, Series GE 87, No. 1, as reported in *Statistical Abstract of the United States* (1990), p. 300, Table 488.

3. Data here are from the *1987 Census of Service Industries*, except for public radio and television, which are from *Statistical Abstract of the United States*, 1990, p. 553. Employment figures for public radio and television are not available.

4. These figures are probably an understatement of the relative position of nonprofits in live theatrical production because the way the Census of Service Industries reports its data makes it impossible to differentiate nonprofit live theatrical production establishments from nonprofit establishments providing other theatrical services. If we assume that 90 percent of the nonprofit theatrical production and theatrical services establishments are in fact live theatrical production companies, then the nonprofit share of this industry is about 52 percent of the establishments and 65 percent of the employment.

5. Based on an estimate of the number of publicly operated museums derived from Paul DiMaggio, "Nonprofit Orga-

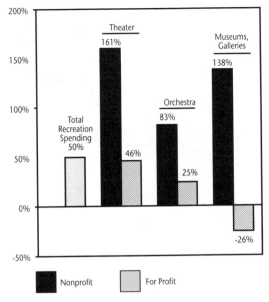

FIGURE 8.4
Recent Trends in Nonprofit and For-Profit Arts and Culture Organization Employment, 1977–87*

*Excludes motion pictures and sports and recreation
Source: 1987 and 1977 *Census of Services Industries.*

"Although the recreation and entertainment industry as a whole is dominated by for-profit providers, nonprofit organizations are clearly the primary producers of live cultural entertainment—theater, symphonic music, opera, galleries, and museums."

nizations in the Production and Distribution of Culture," in Walter Powell, ed. *The Nonprofit Sector: A Research Handbook* (New Haven: Yale University Press, 1987), p. 198.

6. Computed from data in Hodgkinson, Weitzman, et al. (1992), p. 147. That nonprofit arts and culture organizations receive considerable income in the form of works of art and endowment support is evident in the fact that the disparity between total revenue and operating expenditures is higher for arts and culture nonprofits than for any other type. Thus, total revenue is 80 percent higher than operating expenditures for nonprofit arts and culture organizations compared to 25 percent for all nonprofits as of 1989. Assuming the disparity between total revenue and operating expenditures is largely accounted for by such private gifts, private giving accounted for 63 percent of total arts and culture organization revenue in 1987, but only 32 percent of operating spending. That the estimates of the components of operating support reported in the text are roughly accurate seems clear from data generated by the organizations representing several of these types of institutions. Thus, the Association of Art Museum Directors reported that private giving accounted for 27 percent of revenues in 1990. Comparable figures for opera companies, theater, and symphonies were 38 percent, 31 percent, and 46 percent, respectively. From *Giving USA*, 1991, pp. 165-168.

7. Data here are from the *U.S. Census of Service Industries* (1987). Motion picture and sports and recreation are excluded. This picture would differ only slightly if we were to focus on revenues instead of employment.

CHAPTER NINE

Advocacy, Legal Services and International Aid

Important as the nonprofit sector is in the provision of various services—from health and education to arts and culture—it also plays other, possibly even more important, roles as well.

This chapter examines two of the most fundamental of these other roles: first, the nonprofit role in *policy advocacy*, the representation of views or interests, particularly public interests, in the shaping of public policy; and second, the nonprofit role in *international assistance*, the effort to relieve suffering and promote economic growth in less developed countries. In both, the nonprofit sector makes unique, and quite substantial, contributions.

Nonprofit Advocacy Activity

Advocacy, the representation of interests and concerns, usually in the political process, is one of the most distinctive functions of the nonprofit sector. Nonprofits, in this sense, embody one of the most cherished values in American life: the right of free expression and its corollary, the right of association to give effective voice to common concerns.

Private Interest Advocacy

The nonprofit role in advocacy is most highly developed within the member-serving segment of the nonprofit sector. Most of the nearly 60,000 nonprofit, business and professional associations in the United States devote at least a part of their efforts toward the representation and promotion of the interests and views of their business or profession in the political process. They do this by contributing to political campaigns, conducting research on issues affecting their members, testifying before Congress and state legislatures, and presenting the views of their constituencies to political leaders, the press, and the general public

"Advocacy, the representation of interests and concerns, usually in the political process, is one of the most distinctive functions of the nonprofit sector."

97

in dozens of different ways.

As the scope of government involvement in national life has grown, so too has the scope and density of private interest representation, particularly in the nation's capital. The Washington, D.C., telephone directory alone contains close to ten pages of listings of national association or American association of this or that, beginning with the American Advertising Association and ending with the National Wool Growers Association (see Table 9.1). Few facets of national economic or professional life are not represented by at least one, and usually more than one, business or professional association. Indeed, so pervasive has the representation of interests become that some observers despair about the impact that this "interest group liberalism" has on the national capacity to formulate and implement meaningful national policy.[1]

Public Interest Advocacy

More important for our purposes than this extensive advocacy activity on the part of nonprofit business and professional associations is the advocacy activity of *public-serving* nonprofit organizations. Indeed, a whole class of public-interest advocacy organizations has emerged in recent decades specializing in the identification, analysis, and development of potential solutions to public, or community, problems. Beyond this, however, numerous public-benefit service agencies (e.g., social service providers) include advocacy as a significant aspect of their activity, or belong to regional or national associations that advocate on behalf of the clients that the agencies serve.

Given its different forms, it is difficult to be very precise about the exact scope of this public-interest advocacy activity. What we do know, however, is the following:

- **Nonprofit role in recent social movement activity.** The nonprofit sector has been the principal vehicle for most of the major social movements that have emerged in the United States over the past several decades—the civil rights movement, the environmental movement, the consumer movement, the women's rights movement, the abortion rights movement, the antiabortion movement, the gay rights movement, and many more. The sector has thus functioned as a safety valve for public concerns and a mechanism for mobilizing public action and attention on matters of public importance.

- **Nonprofit political action [501(c)(4)] organizations.** To some extent, this advocacy activity takes place through specially organized nonprofit advo-

"The nonprofit sector has been the principal vehicle for most of the major social movements that have emerged in the United States over the past several decades...."

TABLE 9.1

Illustrative Washington-Based Nonprofit Business and Professional Associations

American Apparel Manufacturers Association
American Association for Adult and
   Continuing Education
American Association of Advertising Agencies
American Association of Crop Insurers
American Association of Motor Vehicle
   Administrators
American Bankers Association
American Concrete Pipe Association
American Electronics Association
American Gear Manufacturers Association
American Hardware Manufacturers Association
American Hotel and Motel Association
American Low Power Television Association
American Road and Transportation
   Builders Association
American Sugarbeet Growers Association
National Asphalt Pavement Association
National Association for Hospital
   Admitting Managers
National Association of Beverage Importers
National Association of Broadcasters
National Association of Insurance Brokers
National Association of Scissors and
   Shears Manufacturers
National Association of Manufacturers
National Congress of Petroleum Retailers
National Food Processors Association
National Wooden Pallet and Container
   Association
National Wool Growers Association

Source: C&P Telephone, *District of Columbia White Pages* (1990).

cacy organizations, many of which are organized under Section 501(c)(4) of the Internal Revenue Code. This section of the code is specifically earmarked for public-benefit organizations that wish to engage extensively in lobbying and other political advocacy activities that other public-benefit nonprofits granted tax exemption under section 501(c)(3) of the tax code cannot do as a "substantial part" of their activities.[2] Close to 140,000 such 501(c)(4) organizations were registered with the Internal Revenue Service as of 1987.

- **Advocacy activity by other nonprofits.** Notwithstanding the provisions of the Internal Revenue Code, a considerable amount of public-benefit advocacy takes place through 501(c)(3) organizations, so long as it is not a "substantial part" of these organizations' activity. A recent survey of nonprofit human service and arts organizations found that while only 4 percent of the organizations are *principally* involved in advocacy, about one-fourth of them take part in advocacy activities at least to some extent.[3] This includes research, information development, information sharing, identification of public problems, work with the press, and so forth. Because the scale of the nonprofit sector has grown considerably in the past three decades, this translates into a considerable advocacy force.

- **Specialized national advocacy organizations.** Whether they are organized as 501(c)(3)'s or 501(c)(4)'s, a considerable number of specialized public-interest advocacy organizations have taken their place in Washington, D.C., along with the more numerous private-interest organizations. Some of these represent other nonprofit organizations, such as the American Association of Museums or the National Assembly of National Voluntary Health and Social Welfare Organizations. Others, however, represent otherwise unrepresented or underrepresented groups or perspectives, such as the American Association of Retired Persons, the American Diabetes Association, the American Digestive Disease Society, or the National Association for Music Therapy (see Table 9.2).

- **Neighborhood associations.** In addition to the national or state-oriented advocacy activity, a great deal of advocacy activity also takes place through nonprofit neighborhood organizations. Many of these organizations are informal neighborhood clubs that serve social as well as civic functions. But many are formally incorporated nonprofit organizations functioning to help develop housing and jobs in local areas. These latter were encouraged by the antipoverty program of the mid-1960s,

"...about one-fourth of [of the nation's nonprofit human service agencies] take part in advocacy activities at least to some extent."

TABLE 9.2
Selected Washington-Based Public Interest Advocacy Organizations

Accuracy in Media
American Conservative Union
Americans for Democratic Action
Common Cause
Federation for American Immigration Reform
National Abortion Rights Action League
National Coalition to Ban Handguns
National Right to Life Committee
American Civil Liberties Union
Consumer Federation of America
Independent Sector
National Association of Railroad Passengers
National Urban Coalition
Migrant Legal Action Program
National Council of Negro Women
Environmental Law Institute
Conservation Foundation
National Wildlife Federation
The Nature Conservancy

Source: *Washington '88: A Comprehensive Directory of the Key Institutions and Leaders of the National Capital Area*, edited by J. Russell, A. O'Shea, B. Bachman (Washington: Columbia Books, Inc., 1988).

which fostered the creation of Community Action Agencies involving the participation of the poor; and by the federal Community Development Program, which also encouraged the formation of neighborhood organizations to help oversee the process of community development in inner-city neighborhoods. These organizations often provide an effective mechanism for neighborhood involvement in local decision making. The Planning Department of the City of Baltimore, Maryland, for example, maintains a register of over 600 neighborhood or community organizations in the city that are regularly consulted on property development and other issues in their areas.[4]

Legal Service Organizations

One of the more important facets of public-interest policy advocacy by nonprofit organizations during the past two decades has been the use of the legal system to promote policy changes, and the emergence of specialized nonprofit, public-interest legal organizations in such fields as environmental protection, civil rights, consumer rights, and the like. Many of these organizations were specially created to pursue public-interest policy change through legal action. Others grew out of the efforts sparked by the antipoverty program of the 1960s to make legal services available to the poor and were funded largely by government legal service programs.

Thanks to a Supreme Court ruling in 1966, which changed the definition of "standing" in certain legal cases, it became possible for these public-interest legal organizations to bring cases not only on behalf of particular injured individuals, but also on behalf of entire classes of similarly situated individuals. This made it possible to claim sufficient damages to warrant the costs of a case even though the damages sustained by any individual member of the affected group may have been relatively small.

As shown in Table 9.3, there were 1,439 nonprofit legal service organizations in the United States in 1987, with revenues of $665 million and over 16,000 employees. This represents an increase of almost a third in both organizations and employees over a decade earlier.

How many of these organizations are principally engaged in policy advocacy and class-action law as opposed to more traditional legal services (e.g., divorces, wills, property settlements) is difficult to say. During the 1970s, major efforts were made by the Nixon administration to restrict the advocacy work of the federally funded legal service organizations and limit them to more traditional legal services. Cutbacks

"...a considerable number of specialized public-interest advocacy organizations have taken their place in Washington, D.C., over the past several decades along with the more numerous private-interest organizations."

"One of the more important facets of public-interest policy advocacy by nonprofit organizations during the past two decades has been...the emergence of specialized nonprofit, public-interest legal organizations...."

in the funding of these services during the Reagan administration further hampered their efforts. At the same time, privately funded legal action on behalf of women, minorities, and the environment gained increased support. Many of the issue organizations noted in Table 9.2, in fact, are significantly involved in legal action as a part of their general policy advocacy mission.

Nonprofit Foreign Assistance

Nonprofit organizations also play an important role in international relief and development activities. As of October 30, 1990, for example, there were 277 private, voluntary organizations registered with the U.S. Agency for International Development as available to provide international relief and development assistance. These organizations had revenues that year totalling $4.2 billion.[5] By comparison, U.S. government development assistance has been running about $10 billion per year. Nonprofit foreign assistance activity is thus nearly half that of the U.S. government.

As is the case with domestic nonprofit organizations, however, not all of the revenue that private, nonprofit foreign assistance organizations spend comes from private giving. On the contrary, the same widespread pattern of government-nonprofit cooperation that is evident on the domestic scene also operates in U.S. nonprofit activities abroad.

Thus, as Figure 9.1 shows, 28 percent of the income of nonprofit foreign aid organizations came from government as of 1990. A significant portion of this takes the form of so-called P.L. 480 surplus food made available for distribution through private voluntary organizations. Private giving provided 54 percent of total income, of which about a fifth took the form

FIGURE 9.1
Sources of Nonprofit Foreign Aid Organization Income, 1990

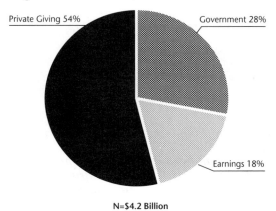

Private Giving 54%   Government 28%   Earnings 18%

N=$4.2 Billion

Source: U.S. Agency for International Development, *Voluntary Foreign Aid Programs, 1991.*

"Nonprofit organizations are also active in the international sphere, extending the reach of traditional government-to-government relief and development aid...."

TABLE 9.3
Nonprofit Legal Service Organizations

Dimension	1977	1987	% Change 1977–87
Establishments	1,101	1,439	+31%
Revenues (millions, 1987 $)	$450	$665	+48
Employees	12,400	16,191	+31

Source: *1977 and 1987 Census of Service Industries.*

of in-kind contributions and the balance cash contributions. Earnings from sales generated an additional 18 percent.

This pattern differed considerably, of course, among different agencies. Most of the larger, private development agencies rely more heavily on government support. Thus, as Figure 9.2 shows, Catholic Relief Services got 72 percent of its total income from government in 1990, CARE received 77 percent, Lutheran World Relief received 58 percent, and the Save the Children Federation received 54 percent. Nevertheless, these organizations provide a vehicle to combine public and private aid, and to reach clientele that might have been difficult for government agencies to approach.

"[Nonprofit organizations] function as critical vehicles of civic action, ensuring a free and open 'civil society' in which different groupings of individuals can make their views known in the policy process...."

Conclusion

Beyond their significant domestic service roles, American nonprofit organizations thus play other vital functions in American national life. For one thing, they function as critical vehicles of civic action, ensuring a free and open "civil society" in which different groupings of individuals can make their views known

FIGURE 9.2
Sources of Income of Selected Nonprofit Foreign Aid Organizations

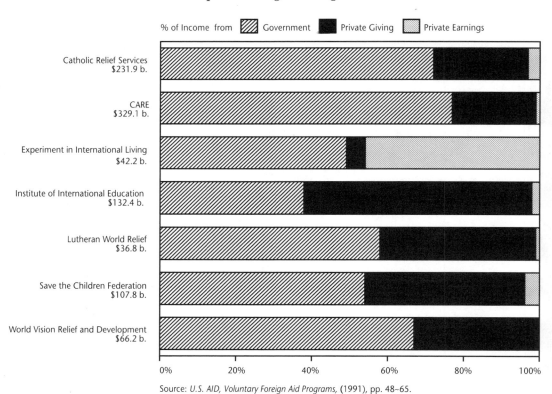

Source: *U.S. AID, Voluntary Foreign Aid Programs,* (1991), pp. 48–65.

in the policy process at both the national and local levels. Nonprofit organizations are in this sense "empowering" institutions, providing a mechanism for joint action on behalf of even the least well-represented groups or views.

In addition, however, nonprofit organizations are also active in the international sphere, extending the reach of traditional, government-to-government relief and development aid, and mobilizing considerable quantities of private resources as well.

ENDNOTES

1. Theodore Lowi, *The End of Liberalism* (New York: W. W. Norton, 1979).

2. As Chapter Two noted, "charitable" organizations that are granted tax-exempt status under Section 501(c)(3) of the Internal Revenue Code are prohibited from "carrying on propaganda, or otherwise to influence legislation" as a "substantial part" of their activities. In return, they are eligible to receive tax deductible gifts from the public. Section 501(c)(4) is intended for public-interest-oriented organizations that specifically wish to engage more actively in the political process. However, such organizations, while exempt from taxes themselves, are not eligible to receive tax deductible gifts or foundation grants.

3. Lester M. Salamon, James C. Musselwhite, Jr., and Carol J. DeVita, "Partners in Public Service: Government and the Nonprofit Sector in the American Welfare State," *Working Papers*, Independent Sector Research Forum (1986); and unpublished tabulations of the Salamon/Urban Institute Nonprofit Sector Survey.

4. Baltimore City Department of Planning, *Baltimore City's Community Association Directory* (1991).

5. U.S. Agency for International Development, *Voluntary Foreign Aid Programs, 1991* (Washington: U.S. Agency for International Development, 1991), p. 64.

CHAPTER TEN

Conclusions

Perhaps the central conclusion that flows from this analysis is that private, nonprofit organizations continue to play a significant role in American society despite the expanded role of the state. This runs counter to much conventional wisdom, which has viewed the expansion of government action over the past half-century or more as fundamentally hostile to the preservation of a vibrant private, nonprofit sector. Because of American hostility to centralized government bureaucracies and the presence of significant nonprofit providers in many of the fields that government has entered, government has tended to turn to nonprofit providers to help deliver publicly funded services—in health, education, and social services. As a consequence, the growth of government has helped to expand the nonprofit role, not limit or eliminate it. As a result, nonprofit organizations retain a significant foothold in virtually every sphere of human service, and in many cases have been able to expand their activities as a direct by-product of government involvement.

This situation poses a serious challenge to the traditional terms and concepts commonly used to depict our social welfare system. Although government provides most of the funds in many of the key social welfare fields, private institutions deliver most of the services. Does this make the system public or private? Unfortunately, we do not even have the words to portray the situation. In some fields, such as hospital care, nonprofit organizations clearly play the largest role. In others, such as nursing home care, for-profit institutions are the major providers. Does this make the system mostly philanthropic or mostly commercial? Like the elephant examined by three blind men in the ancient tale, the American social welfare system appears to be a different beast depending on who

"In a sense, Americans have surrendered the comprehensiveness and coherence of the social welfare systems of many European countries for the pluralism and adaptability of a much looser and more diverse system of mixed public and private care."

"Perhaps the central conclusion that flows from this analysis is that private, nonprofit organizations continue to play a significant role in American society despite the expanded role of the state."

touches it and where. It is, in fact, not a single system at all—whether governmental, nonprofit, or for profit—but all three together. If "public-private partnership" is not a perfect way to characterize the reality that exists, it certainly comes closer than any of the other alternative concepts. But even it has limitations, because nonprofit organizations are often in the position of criticizing and prodding government rather than simply cooperating with it to carry out public objectives.

While the "mixed" character of the American social welfare system makes it more difficult to comprehend and explain, it may also make it stronger and more capable of change. In a sense, Americans have surrendered the comprehensiveness and coherence of the social welfare systems of many European countries for the pluralism and adaptability of a much looser and more diverse system of mixed public and private care. In doing so, we have taken on an added challenge of analysis and education to make our complex system comprehensible to our own citizenry and government officials as well as to those interested in comprehending its lessons abroad. Unfortunately, ideological stereotypes and political rhetoric have kept us from meeting this challenge very effectively. If this primer has helped to overcome this problem, at least in part, it will have amply served its purpose.

References

AAFRC Trust for Philanthropy, *Giving USA: 1991* (New York: AAFRC Trust for Philanthropy, 1991).

American Hospital Association, *Hospital Statistics, 1990/91* (Chicago: American Hospital Association, 1990/91).

Bixby, Ann Kallman, "Overview of Public Social Welfare Expenditures, Fiscal Year 1989," *Social Security Bulletin*, Vol. 54, No. 10 (November 1991).

Bixby, Ann Kallman, "Public Social Welfare Expenditures, Fiscal Years 1965-87," *Social Security Bulletin*, Vol. 53, No. 2 (February 1991), pp. 1-25.

Bixby, Ann Kalman, "Social Welfare Expenditures, 1963-83," *Social Security Bulletin*, Vol. 49, No. 2 (February 1986), pp. 12-21.

Brenton, Maria, *The Voluntary Sector in British Social Services* (London: Longman, 1985).

Brilliant, Eleanor, *The United Way: Dilemmas of Organized Charity* (New York: Columbia University Press, 1991).

Commission on Philanthropy and Public Needs, *Giving in America: Toward a Stronger Voluntary Sector* (Washington, DC: Commission on Private Philanthropy and Public Needs, 1975).

Council for Aid to Education, *Voluntary Support of Education, 1986-87* (New York: Council for Aid to Education, 1988).

deToqueville, Alexis, *Democracy in America* [The Henry Reeve Text] (New York: Alfred A. Knopf, Inc., 1945).

DiMaggio, Paul, "Nonprofit Organizations in the Production and Distribution of Culture," in W. Powell, ed., (1987).

Foundation Center, *Foundations Today*, 7th ed. Compiled by Loren Renz. (New York: The Foundation

Center, 1990).

Gidron, Benjamin, Ralph Kramer, and Lester M. Salamon, eds. *Government and the Nonprofit Sector: Emerging Relationships in Welfare States* (San Francisco: Jossey-Bass, 1992).

Hansmann, Henry, "Why Are Nonprofit Organizations Exempted from Corporate Income Taxation," in Michelle J. White (ed.), *Nonprofit Firms in a Three-Sector Economy*, COUPE Papers (Washington, DC: The Urban Institute Press, 1981).

Hodgkinson, Virginia, and Murray Weitzman, *Dimensions of the Independent Sector: A Statistical Profile*, 3rd ed. (Washington: Independent Sector, 1989).

Hodgkinson, Virginia A., Murray S. Weitzman, Christopher M. Toppe, and Stephen M. Noga, *Nonprofit Almanac 1992-1993: Dimensions of the Independent Sector* (San Francisco, CA: Jossey-Bass Publishers, Inc., 1992).

Hodgkinson, Virginia A., and Murray S. Weitzman, *Giving and Volunteering in the United States: Findings from a National Survey.* 1990 Edition. (Washington, DC: Independent Sector, 1990).

Hopkins, Bruce R., *The Law of Tax-Exempt Organizations*, 5th ed. (New York: John Wiley and Sons, 1989).

Kramer, Ralph, *Voluntary Agencies in the Welfare State* (Berkeley: University of California Press, 1981).

Lowi, Theodore, *The End of Liberalism* (New York: W.W. Norton, 1979).

National Council of the Churches of Christ In the United States, *Yearbook of American and Canadian Churches* (New York: National Council of the Churches of Christ, 1990).

Nielsen, Waldeman, *The Endangered Sector* (New York: Columbia University Press, 1980).

O'Neill, Michael, *The Third America: The Emergence of the Nonprofit Sector in the United States* (San Francisco: Jossey-Bass Publishers, 1989).

Organization of Economic Cooperation and Development (OECD), *National Accounts, Detailed Tables, 1976-1988* (Paris: OECD, 1991).

Powell, Walter, ed. *The Nonprofit Sector: A Research Handbook* (New Haven: Yale University Press, 1987).

Renz, Loren, *Foundation Giving: Yearbook of Facts and Figures on Private, Corporate, and Community Foundations.* 1991 Edition. (New York: The Foundation Center, 1991).

Russell, J., A. O'Shea, and B. Bachman, eds. *Washington '88: A Comprehensive Directory of the Key Institu-*

tions and Leaders of the National Capital Area (Washington: Columbia Books, Inc., 1988).

Salamon, Lester M. (ed.), *Beyond Privatization: The Tools of Government Action* (Washington: The Urban Institute Press, 1989).

Salamon, Lester M., "Nonprofit Organizations: The Lost Opportunity," in John L. Palmer and Isabel Sawhill, eds., *The Reagan Record*, (Cambridge: Ballinger Publishing Co., 1984), pp. 261-286.

Salamon, Lester M., "Rethinking Public Management: Third-Party Government and the Changing Forms of Government Action," *Public Policy* 29 (1981): 255-275.

Salamon, Lester M., *Welfare: The Elusive Consensus—Where We Are, How We Got Here, and What's Ahead* (New York: Praeger Publishers, 1977).

Salamon, Lester M., and Alan J. Abramson, *The Federal Budget and the Nonprofit Sector* (Washington, DC: The Urban Institute, 1982).

Salamon, Lester M., and Alan J. Abramson, "The Nonprofit Sector." in John L. Palmer and Isabel Sawhill (eds.), *The Reagan Experiment* (Washington, DC: The Urban Institute Press, 1982).

Salamon, Lester M., and Alan J. Abramson, *The Nonprofit Sector and the New Federal Budget* (Washington: The Urban Institute, 1986).

Salamon, Lester M., David M. Altschuler, and Jaana Myllyluoma, *More Than Just Charity: The Baltimore Area Nonprofit Sector in a Time of Change* (Baltimore: The Johns Hopkins Institute for Policy Studies, 1990).

Salamon, Lester M., James C. Musselwhite, Jr., and Carol J. DeVita, "Partners in Public Service: Government and the Nonprofit Sector in the American Welfare State." *Working Papers*, Independent Sector Research Forum, March 1986.

Sirrocco, Al, "Nursing and Related Care Homes as Reported from the 1986 Inventory of Long-Term Care Places," *Advancedata,* No. 147 (January 22, 1988).

U.S. Agency for International Development, *Voluntary Foreign Aid Programs, 1991* (Washington, DC: U.S. Agency for International Development, 1991).

U.S. Bureau of the Census, *1987 Census of Service Industries* (Washington, DC: U.S. Government Printing Office, Nov. 1989).

U.S. Bureau of the Census, *Statistical Abstract of the United States, 1990.* (Washington, DC: U.S. Government Printing Office, 1991).

U.S. Department of Education, National Center for Education Statistics, *Digest of Education Statistics,*

1990 (Washington, DC: U.S. Government Printing Office, 1991).

U.S. Department of Health and Human Services, Public Health Service, *Surgeon General's Workshop on Self-Help and Public Health* (Washington, DC: U.S. Government Printing Office, 1988).

Weisbrod, Burton, *The Voluntary Nonprofit Sector* (Lexington, MA: Lexington Books, 1978).

Whitehead, John S., *The Separation of College and State: Columbia, Dartmouth, Harvard and Yale, 1776-1876* (New Haven, CT: Yale University Press, 1973).

Wolch, Jennifer, *The Shadow State* (New York: The Foundation Center, 1990).